"Process. A power our lives and ministry efforts. Though process may be neglected by many, Pastor DuBose in *The Creator's Wheel* takes you on a journey through God's Word that brings life-changing truth regarding process, present in the nature and plan of God."

Bret L. Allen, district superintendent of Northern
California and Nevada Assemblies of God

"Rick DuBose's insightful and inspirational new book *The Creator's Wheel* is a timely read. It will open your eyes and heart to God's plan and purposes no matter what season of life you find yourself in. This is not just a feel-good book, but a faith-building book. It will help you live as a victor and not a victim."

Dr. Bill and Joy Wilson, pastors, personal
coaches, and national leaders

"Rick DuBose exposits Scripture in such a way that you will be challenged by the sovereign process that God designed to build us into the people He needs and that we want to be. I was moved in every chapter to recognize the greatness of the God of all creation and His reign in my life and ministry. *The Creator's Wheel* will lead you to worship God and His faithfulness in every season of life."

David Ellis, regional director of Assemblies
of God World Missions

Books by Rick DuBose

In Jesus' Name: 5 Altars of Prayer That Move Heaven and Earth
The Creator's Wheel: 7 Phases of Godly Transformation

THE CREATOR'S WHEEL

7 PHASES of GODLY TRANSFORMATION

RICK DUBOSE

Chosen

a division of Baker Publishing Group
Minneapolis, Minnesota

Published by Chosen Books
Minneapolis, Minnesota
ChosenBooks.com

Chosen Books is a division of
Baker Publishing Group, Grand Rapids, Michigan

Printed in the United States of America

Library of Congress Cataloging-in-Publication Data
Names: DuBose, Rick, author.
Title: The creator's wheel : 7 phases of godly transformation / Rick DuBose.
Description: Minneapolis, Minnesota : Chosen Books, a division of Baker
    Publishing Group, [2025]
Identifiers: LCCN 2024017787 | ISBN 9780800763664 (paper) | ISBN 9780800773045
    (casebound) | ISBN 9781493443987 (ebook)
Subjects: LCSH: Creation. | Holy Spirit. | Bible--Verses.
Classification: LCC BL227 .D74 2025 | DDC 231.7/65--dc23/eng/20240705
LC record available at https://lccn.loc.gov/2024017787

Cover design by InsideOut Creative Arts, Inc.

Baker Publishing Group publications use paper produced from sustainable forestry practices and postconsumer waste whenever possible.

25   26   27   28   29   30   7   6   5   4   3   2   1

Contents

FOREWORD

The doctrine of creation endures as a bedrock doctrine in Christianity. Believing that God created the world teaches us something vital about God, about the world, and about ourselves. We learn to worship God as creator. We learn to appreciate the world as a gift. We learn our place within this world as the image of God. The Christian doctrine of creation guides our worship of God, our faith in God, and our obedience to God.

The belief that God created the world can be found in multiple places in the Old Testament including Genesis 1–2, Job 38–41, Psalm 33:6–9, Psalm 104, and Proverbs 8:22–31. In each chapter, the point is not to narrate an exact timeline or the same series of events leading to creation, but to show the relationship between God as creator of the world and the need of the reader or audience today. Job 38–41 says suffering, like creation, is mysterious, but God stays in control of it all. The promise of Psalm 33:6–9 is that the God who spoke creation into existence can rescue His people.

The most famous account of creation, Genesis 1, describes creation as an act of God who turns chaos into cosmos. Creation results from God's ordering or separating light from dark, waters above from waters below, and water from land, before God fills what was separated with all that is needed for life. This text, serving as an introduction to Genesis, prepares the reader for God's ongoing presence in the world through the generations leading to Abraham and beyond. God is faithful and remains committed to whatever God created. As sole creator, God perpetuates and preserves what and who God created. Because God is our creator, we can trust in God as our Savior.

The Creator's Wheel, which came out of Rick DuBose's devotional time, offers a devotional reading of Genesis 1 as an illustration of the divine process in transforming chaos into cosmos in every person. The promise offered by this kind of reading is what God did for creation and what God will do for us, making something beautiful out of the chaos of our lives.

Rick DuBose is not the first person to make a connection between the creation story in Genesis 1 and the salvific work of God among His people. This will be the first time, though, when many readers make that connection. DuBose does not write as a Bible scholar, as a scientist, or as someone pushing a version of creationism. He writes as a pastor with years of experience in successfully guiding the spiritual development of individuals and congregations. If he has found Genesis 1 useful in illustrating a process of spiritual formation, so will the reader.

I have had the privilege of watching Rick DuBose work for some time. He is enthusiastic about creating spiritually healthy churches that create spiritually healthy disciples. The development of spiritual health involves prayer, godly leadership, and robust processes properly aligned with the word of God. Along with his earlier books on prayer and church authority, *The Creator's Wheel* explains how the Holy Spirit makes the difference in persons and communities, leading them to reflect the image of Christ.

This book encourages us to trust in the process of the Spirit's work in our lives based on Genesis 1. We need to be reminded of the importance of creation in understanding salvation. Without the doctrine of creation, we are left adrift in a humanity we do not understand or appreciate. We share no story of our beginnings or purpose, and we are left uncertain as to our ending. Without an understanding of God as creator, we cannot imagine ourselves as creations of God.

All we are left with is to imagine ourselves as accidents of nature, self-made gods, or both. Each view endangers our spiritual development. It is no wonder that, as our culture moves further into a post-Christian era, we cannot agree on the most basic truths about humanity. In time of cultural divisiveness and confusion, we need the Christian doctrine of creation more than ever.

Dr. Allen Tennsion, theological counsel to the
General Council of the Assemblies of God

Author's Note

As I worked through Genesis in my daily devotions, I began to realize that the creation account is more than a story about the world being formed. It is an explanation of *how* God creates. In Genesis, we not only see the world formed, but we also see the creative process God used to form it. Through His process of creation, we discover who the creator is. I began to wonder if Genesis might reveal how God works beyond Genesis. Might God's process of creation be playing out in all history and in each of our individual lives as well? What if Genesis was given to help us better understand how God is creating new things in us even now? What if the opening chapters of Genesis teach us not only what God did, but also what He is currently doing?

It's not hard to see in our own lives and history the same dark chaos from which creation was drawn. God often meets us and begins His transformative work by drawing us out of similar darkness and chaotic situations. Seeing this reality, I quickly began to recognize patterns in the other days of creation: light, atmosphere, structure, dominion, and rest. God was intentional about how He created, and I began to recognize those same patterns in how He formed His people, Israel, and how He is still forming churches and followers today.

As a pastor, I began to show these patterns to the men and women in my congregation. They recognized them in their own lives as easily as I had my own. Seeing how God was working in Genesis gave them faith to see God working that same process in their darkness and chaos. Our church experienced an outpouring of faith and hope. We were learning to trust God's process instead of demanding He follow ours.

We are all tempted to rush God. We want Him to answer our prayers this instant. We want things to happen now, and we grow impatient waiting. We grow unnerved when we do not see the change we want. For all of God's miraculous interventions, which I firmly believe He still does, God's foundational way of transforming things is process. From the seven days of creation to the three days the world waited for Christ's resurrection, we are called to learn and trust His process.

I hope this book will serve as an introduction to that process of creation, but more than that, I hope it will also build your faith. I hope it will help you learn to recognize how God is already at work in your life, creating new things. Don't be in a hurry. Listen to the Spirit as you read. God has something to say to you beyond the words I have written. We will spend much time looking at the physical creation of the world, but this book is about God Himself. And it is about how God is at work right now in your life. I can't wait for you to discover what He is already creating in you. Trust His process, and you will see why God called each day's work good. He has good things already forming in your life.

INTRODUCTION

Every family, company, and person have a way of getting things done. If you take a job at a new employer, one of the first things you'll have to learn is how that company works. You'll have to learn their ways. Knowing what you have been hired to accomplish is only part of the equation. You'll have to learn how things get done. If you refuse to learn, you'll quickly be frustrated with your boss, fellow employees, and that new job.

God also has a way of getting things done. His kingdom has a culture, a process, and a way of working in this world. If you decide to follow God but fail to learn the ways He works, you will soon become frustrated and discouraged by God as well. It's not enough to understand the way your family has done it or the way your religious community works. What matters above all else is that you learn how God's ways. As God Himself reminds us in Isaiah 55:9, "As the heavens are higher than the earth, so are my ways higher than your ways and my thoughts than your thoughts."

Take Moses as your example. At the burning bush, God called him to go and deliver his fellow Hebrews who were enslaved by Egypt. But Moses realized that goal wasn't enough. He needed to know God, and he needed to know God's ways. In Exodus 33:12–13 Moses prays to God, "You have been telling me, 'Lead these people,' but you have not let me know whom you will send with me . . . If you are pleased with me, teach me your ways so I may know you and continue to find favor with you." Moses recognized that holding on to God's promise wasn't enough. Moses wanted to live and act in coordination with the ways of God's process.

God answered Moses' prayers. He showed Moses not only His miraculous power but also His process and the ways in which He worked. Psalm 103:7 records, "He made known his ways to Moses, his deeds to the people of Israel." Moses was given a greater gift than even God's people. While the people saw God's deeds, Moses saw God's ways.

It takes work to understand God's ways. God works by a process and timing often different from the world's. How do we understand His ways when they are so far beyond our own? The apostle Paul answered this question, writing to the Romans, "Do not conform to the patterns of this world but be transformed by the renewing of your mind. Then you will be able to test and approve what God's will is—his good, pleasing, and perfect will" (11:3).

God wants to do great things in your life, but even more than that, He wants to teach you His ways. As with Moses, when you conform your lives to His ways and not the world's, you find God's favor in new ways. Together, I want to look beneath the deeds of God and peer into God's ways. If you humble yourself and quiet your heart, God will show it to you.

When you understand His ways and submit your life to His creative process, you will experience God's favor in profoundly new ways. Let me show you.

THE POWER OF PROCESS

But the LORD made the earth by his power,
 and he preserves it by his wisdom.
With his own understanding
 he stretched out the heavens. . . .
The whole human race is foolish and has no
 knowledge!
 The craftsmen are disgraced by the idols they
 make,
for their carefully shaped works are a fraud.
 These idols have no breath or power. . . .
But the God of Israel is no idol!
 He is the Creator of everything that exists.
 —Jeremiah 10:12, 14, 16 NLT

God is a creator. It's the first word we learn about Him from Scripture. "In the beginning God created" (Genesis 1:1). It was His first act, His first expression of who He is.

God began His self-revelation by creating. We shouldn't rush past that word. It is the first thing we learn about God. He creates. The false gods of the ancient world were not called creators. They were formed by human hands and demonically inspired imagination. Worshiping them led to war, violence, and destruction. The true and living God, the God of the Bible, was not made with human hands, nor was He something that came from someone's imagination. Rather, He is the creator of everything that exists, both natural and supernatural. Everything came from His unlimited and unimaginable intelligence. In the beginning, God created!

The Bible, therefore, opens with a powerful word of God's decisive action. God, by His character and decree, created the heavens and the earth. Day by day, God added to His creation, layering on more complexity and detail. With each day, His creation expanded into that final work by which He formed man in His own image and placed humanity in the center of His masterpiece. It was good. That's how God described it. And the world He created reflected His goodness. The heavens and the earth declared His glory. And on the final day, God rested.

The leaders of Jesus' day—the patriarchs, the prophets, the poets, and Jesus Himself—recognized God's role as creator. They recognized the revelation of His glory that poured from it. It was His word that stretched out the sky. It was His hand that knit us together in the womb. It was His divine design by which all things came to be. God created; that is the first word we learn about God. But that is not the only word. We are also told *how* God created. God created the heavens and earth through an intentional process.

God could have spoken the heavens and earth into existence with a single word on a single day. He could have spoken, and all of it would have existed in an instant. He did not need seven days in which to do His work. All things could have existed in a single moment. But that is not how Genesis records it. God, for all His creative power, intentionally chose to work through seven days of creation. God worked in seven creative stages. Our world exists because of that process. And it's in that process you can begin to better understand how God continues to work in your life.

God chose to start the story of our journey with Him focusing on a dark, non-producing mess. If we had been there—rather than us being on the other end, the completed end of what He was about to do—we would have seen the situation as hopeless and formidable. But the story quickly points out and declares that His Spirit was already hovering over it, brooding and incubating it, even before He spoke to it. God had a plan for it even while it was shrouded in darkness.

Before He created the earth and mankind, before sin entered and started its work of destruction, before we could know what we would need from Him, God was already showing us that He is a God who has unlimited ability to restore, heal, redeem, and turn messes into masterpieces. And He was now about to reveal the step-by-step process He would use to do it. He was about to show us how He would turn the messes that would be caused by sin into something very good.

———

The world was formless. It was chaos. When God looked into the emptiness and saw the mess, He saw a canvas upon which He would act to bring about creation. But that work began in the chaos of emptiness. God initiated His process of creation from the void the way a painter layers color upon color. Each day He would introduce a new function until each function was layered upon the other functions. Once everything needed to change the mess and sustain it until all that God intended could be accomplished was created, He backed up, looked at it, and said, "It is very good."

The functions:

- **Day 1—Revelation:** God spoke, and light broke through the darkness. By His word of revelation, God brought vision and clarity to the chaos.
- **Day 2—Atmosphere:** He created an expanse over the waters. God formed the environment necessary for the life that would soon fill the space.
- **Day 3—Structure:** God separated the water from the sky and pulled the ground up from the depths. God separated the spaces into structured order. Each space took on its proper form.
- **Day 4—Seasons:** God formed the repeating cycles of time and seasons. These seasons prepared the ground and sky for the cycles of life to come. Man and beast would learn to live in the seasons of His design.
- **Day 5—Addition:** God placed fish in the sea and birds in the air. He began with those animals that

are separate from the ground, those that pass beneath us and above us.

- **Day 6—Opposition and Authority:** He created beasts, and He drew up man from the dust. He gave man the task of naming, ruling, and shepherding. He called humanity to take up the responsibility of stewarding creation within His process. He gave humanity a divine task.

- **Day 7—Rest:** God looked on what He had created and called it good. His process had brought about His vision. His process had, with time, fulfilled His design.

What His Process Reveals

Most are familiar with the days of creation. Many of us learned them as children, and some of our greatest scientific minds have worked to unpack their logic and the evidence of God's creative work through them. Genesis chapter one is often debated and discussed. We form theories and arguments. We look for evidence. But God's days of creation are not merely scientific. Neither are they merely poetic. We should ask why. Why, with His power to have created by any means, did God choose to use a process of seven days? Why did God choose to create through these seven distinct stages? What did God seek to reveal about Himself in that process?

God chose His process for a reason. He designed our world by that process so that we might learn to recognize how He uses that same process in our lives. God used this process because He continues to work in our lives by those same creative stages. He created in seven stages for our sake. He's still working through those stages.

The apostle Paul wrote to the Ephesians, "We are God's masterpiece. He has created us anew in Christ Jesus, so we can do the good things he planned for us long ago" (2:10 NLT). What Paul recognized was that the same God who created the world also works to form us into a new creation. It's the same creative work, now being done in us, to make us more like Christ. God is the same yesterday and today. He is still using His creative process to bring about our restoration and to change our life and world.

God uses a process because that process also reveals things about who He is. It's always the process of creators that allows us to recognize their work. It's true of writers. No writer thinks a book into existence. He or she must work through a long process: outlines, drafts, edits, design, and layout. What makes a writer is his or her process. It's true of all artists and creators.

Occasionally the news will report about a new painting from a famous artist being discovered in someone's attic or in some lost archive. Imagine finding a great work by Rembrandt or Van Gogh that was left decades ago in a dusty corner of your attic. Wiping the dust from the edge of the painting and seeing that famous artist's signature, you might think you hit the jackpot. Those paintings can be worth millions of dollars. But the finished painting is not enough. The signature is not enough. The painting must be authenticated by an expert. It takes someone who has studied that artist to validate that the work is real and not a fake. How do experts study the authenticity of a painting? They study and learn to recognize the artist's process. We know an artist by his or her process of creation.

Some painters begin by rough sketching on the canvas. Other painters use a big brush and start blocking in color. An expert will use equipment like an X-ray machine to look through the layers of paint and varnish to uncover the artist's first strokes. They will compare what they observe with other known works of that painter. They'll look for patterns in the supplies used and the technique visible in the brush strokes. What marks a painter is his or her process. If you want to understand artists and recognize their work, you have to understand their process.

We can learn to recognize the creative work of God in our lives by recognizing His process. We can learn to recognize where He is at work, and we can learn how to spot fakes. Genesis gives us a clear and powerful picture of how God works. We get to observe His creative process on a massive scale. If we pay close attention, we can observe not only what He created but how He did it and how He continues to work. We can learn the process by which God is working in our lives right now.

The Process Is the Story

When you learn to recognize God's creative process in Genesis, you soon discover those same creative patterns throughout the whole biblical story. Just as artists might use their signature technique on very different sized canvases, God also uses His process of creation both in the large scale of redemptive history and the individual scale of each human life. God's creative process is at work in your life right now. You need only learn to recognize it.

Consider how God worked in the lives of Adam and Eve. He warned them that if they ate of the forbidden fruit they would die. But having eaten the fruit, they did not die immediately. Why not? God could have buried them in the garden and used their graves as a warning to the next humans He created from the ground. Hopefully, with the warning of Adam and Eve's failure, they could have avoided the serpent's temptation. But God chose instead to expel Adam and Eve and to allow the consequences of their disobedience to play out over years.

Adam and Eve stepped out of the garden into wilderness chaos with only their lives and the seeds of a once-flourishing garden. God made them a promise. One day, an offspring of Adam and Eve would crush the head of the serpent that had deceived them. Like the chaos of darkness from which God began, Adam and Eve stepped out into a disordered and broken world. But they took with them a promise, a light of revelation. God would now begin a new work, a process of redemption and salvation. He would form a new creation out of failure. God would restore all that had been lost, but it would not happen in a moment. His restoration would come through a process.

We are still in that process. Through Christ, salvation comes in a single moment of faith and confession—but the process of conforming our lives into that salvation, into something Christlike, takes time. God works in our lives through His process. That process can be hard to recognize and hard to understand. Moses, called to lead God's people through the process of wilderness wandering, prayed to God, "Let me know your ways so I may understand you more fully" (Exodus 33:13 NLT). What Moses recognized was that God's ways are not our ways. His process is not always our process. We have to learn to recognize how God works to understand what He is doing in us.

Most of us expect God to act now. We have a vision we want to see Him accomplish today. We pray for it to be done this moment. We want our churches changed. We want our lives fixed. We want our world restored. We want God to do it now. We imagine the masterpiece He is painting and are impatient to see it finished. We become confused when God takes out His tools and begins stretching the canvas and priming it with paint. We imagine He isn't working simply because we don't recognize the stage we're in. We don't understand His process of creation, and so we struggle to recognize how He is preparing us for what He still has to come.

Temptation Grows in Impatience

A process requires patience, and patience doesn't come naturally to us. Our world is speeding up. Industrialization and technology have given us the power to do more in shorter periods of time. We grow impatient waiting any more than two days for our packages to be delivered. We expect our food to be fast, our travel to be efficient, and our access to anything immediate.

Those who work in business know the importance of efficiency. There's money to be made in getting the job done more quickly. If you can cut steps out of the process, you win. We're all looking for shortcuts and life hacks to squeeze out any margins we can find. We want as short a process as possible. Naturally, our prayer lives turn into searching for these same shortcuts. We pray with a final image in mind and grow impatient with anything less. Perhaps worse, our impatience often leads us into temptation.

All temptation grows out of impatience. Every temptation is a form of short-cutting the process God is working. We want what God has promised, but we want it by our own means and in our own timing. Think again about the temptations Jesus faced in the wilderness. He had gone through forty days of fasting. He was alone and hungry. So, Satan's first temptation was an encouragement for Jesus to turn stones into bread to fill His stomach. Satan tempted Jesus to grow impatient with His hunger and to use His power for His own gain. In his second temptation, Satan suggested Jesus throw Himself off the temple and allow the angels to rescue Him. It was a temptation to bypass suffering. Finally, Satan asked Jesus to bow to him. In return, he would give Jesus all the power of the world. He painted a final picture of what Jesus could possess and offered Him a shortcut to achieving it without the God-ordered process.

Satan tempted Jesus when He was alone, hungry, tired, and in the wilderness. He tempted Jesus when Jesus might have been most susceptible to giving up on the process and promises. Each temptation was a shortcut. Satan appealed to human impatience. But each time, Jesus refused Satan's offer. Jesus trusted God, but more specifically, Jesus trusted the process God was working. God's word was

His food. He would not test God. God alone would be worshiped. Jesus submitted Himself to the process God was working through Him. He would not be tempted by impatience.

Do you remember in Exodus 32 when the Hebrew people became impatient waiting for Moses to come down from the mountain? For forty days they waited, but Moses did not return. As time passed, they grew restless. They grumbled and complained because they wanted something they could see. They didn't want an invisible God who was taking weeks to reveal His law to Moses. They wanted a god they could control and a god they could possess immediately. They became impatient. So, they took off their gold and convinced Aaron to cast them an idol. They made a golden calf and called it their god. They were tired of waiting.

It was a shortcut, an image, a manmade thing. They rejected God's process. They made a god on their timetable. That act became Scripture's model sin of idolatry. The Old Testament prophets recognized that idols were a distorted creation that denied the creative process of God. Often the prophets mocked the people for carving gods out of stone and wood and imagining they had created a real god. Jeremiah prophesied, "The craftsmen are disgraced by the idols they make, for their carefully shaped works are a fraud" (Jeremiah 10:14 NLT).

Israel's idols were hacks. They were fakes. They were not works of real creation. They were lifeless and worthless imitations of art. They were fake gods that humanity used to bypass God's process of new creation. The apostle Paul wrote to the Romans, "They exchanged the truth about God for a lie, and worshiped and served created things rather than the Creator" (Romans 1:25). It was true of their worship, and it was also true of their patience. They grew impatient and exchanged God's creative process for their own creative shortcuts. The two are never the same. Yet we still face that same old temptation. We still grow impatient and choose our own way.

As a pastor, I've long recognized how destructive impatience can be. We do not want to submit ourselves to a process, and we still look for idolatrous shortcuts to hack out our salvation. Many turn to substances to self-medicate for loss and pain, and the addiction destroys their lives. Some sacrifice the richness of marriage and true love for the cheap thrills of sex and lust. Some steal, forfeiting the treasure of heaven. Some poison their hearts with envy and jealousy. They want for themselves what their neighbor has, and they want it now. Each is a distorted act that breaks God's process.

I have watched families leave a healthy church that is helping them live out their Christian life and raise their children to chase after a job that pays more money. I have seen couples give up on marriages that could have been saved only to wish later they had pushed through. I have watched people chase after position, power, and pleasure only to discover that, without a proper foundation, those things become nothing more than sails to catch the destructive wind of a coming storm. I have had people cry in my office because they wished they had been patient with the slower foundation-building process God had them in.

Rather than settle for what we can have now during the God-ordained process, people often chase after a cheap imitation. Instead of waiting for the real thing, we rashly reach for a lie. Our impatience leads us to believe that it's all or nothing—that what God has for us in the future isn't worth waiting for. The more we indulge our impatience, the less we understand or value His process. Our impatience poisons our prayers and blinds us to what God is doing now.

The reason it's important to recognize the stages of God's creative work is so that we can learn to recognize how He is working and what His timing is. Just because we haven't reached the end of the process doesn't mean God has abandoned us. We must learn to understand His process so that we can recognize what He's doing in this stage of His process. We need to learn His process so that we don't grow impatient and miss what He's offering.

By submitting to God's process, Jesus not only received His promised authority over earth, but also over heaven. By submitting to God's process, Jesus redeemed us and is bringing us forward to reign with Him in the New Heaven and New Earth. Our shortcuts and impatience turn our attention to ourselves. They shrink our world and tempt us to settle for far less than God has designed. God's process is always about more than just us. His process leads to what is very good for us, for our families, for our neighbors, and for all creation.

Learning to recognize the creative stages of God's process not only frees you from the temptations of impatience, but it also helps you make the most out of what God is currently doing in your life.

Benefits of Knowing His Process

Learning the process of God's creation will have several benefits on your life and leadership.

Know Your Creator

God's character is revealed through His process. Learning to see God's stages of creation will help you know God better. God is not the author of confusion. He is a God of order and structure. He has worked in the lives of men and women before you, and by their stories, you can discern how He is at work in your life. The more you know God, the more you learn to trust Him. You learn that His process is good and what He creates by it is good.

Build Your Faith

Learning the stages of God's process builds your faith. It allows you to recognize the stage you're in, and it allows you to appreciate where you've been and where God is leading you. You are not lost wandering in meaninglessness. God is at work. He is creating and restoring. Every day is another opportunity to see His hand at work and, by faith, to participate with Him.

Partner with Him

Recognizing the stage you're in will help you focus your work and prayers. Knowing what God is doing will help you participate in and pray for His will to be done. Each stage is a preparation for the stages that follow. Instead of fighting against God's work, you can learn to partner with Him to make the most of each creative stage.

Worship God

Every stage of God's process is a miracle. Every stage is reason to worship. The psalms recognize that each day of creation glorifies God. The sky declares His goodness. The depths of the sea, the rising and setting sun, and the diversity of the plants and animals all demonstrate His glory. I don't want my life to rush past what God is doing. I don't want to miss all the good things He is doing in and around me. I want a spiritual awareness that allows me to give thanks for every miraculous stage of creation He is working in my life. I want to learn to worship Him in each stage of His creative work.

God's creative process reveals who He is, and recognizing it moves us to greater faith and worship.

———

I believe this book can change your life. Not because it holds secrets or shortcuts, but because it will help you recognize what God is already at work doing. It will change your life by inviting you into the creative work of God.

Following God is a process. Experiencing all He has for you requires a process. But He is the greatest creator, capable of doing more in your life than you could ever do on your own. He longs to turn your mess into a masterpiece. He longs to lead you through His process, forming and shaping your life into all the goodness He has designed for you. It will take patience, and it will take submission to His process, but trust that God has more for you. Do not grow weary. Do not give up. Do not settle for less.

By faith, learn and grow and receive. See God at work in ways you've overlooked. No mess is beyond His salvation. No life is beyond His power to re-create. God is at work in your life right now. Can you see it? Can you recognize it? Can you welcome the stages of His creative process in your life?

> The heavens proclaim the glory of God.
> The skies display his craftsmanship.
> Day after day they continue to speak;
> night after night they make him known.
>
> Psalm 19:1–2 NLT

Chaos and Darkness

> Now the earth was formless and empty, darkness was over the surface of the deep, and the Spirit of God was hovering over the waters.
>
> —Genesis 1:2

Before there was a garden, before there was man or woman, before there was a sun and moon, there was emptiness. Creation began in a state of darkness. The earth was formless. Many translations use the word *void*. There was no meaning. There was no significance. It was only chaos. That chaos was also covered by darkness. There was no opposition to the darkness. The darkness ruled over the emptiness, and it covered the deep.

Those elements—chaos and darkness—would become major themes of the biblical story. It would not be long before the darkness and chaos spread to the human heart. In the book of Genesis, God spoke light into existence to push back the darkness, and He would have to bring that light back to the heart of man. In the Old Testament, He was the flame that did not burn out and the pillar of fire that led through the wilderness. In the Gospels, the light came in the form of man. John recorded Jesus' statement: "I am the light of the world. If you follow me, you won't have to walk in darkness, because you will have the light that leads to life" (John 8:12 NLT). The light continues to build as the Church spreads throughout the world. The light finds its culmination in the image of Revelation in which there will be no darkness at all. There will be no night, for God's light will be unending.

God's story is the story of bringing light and order to the chaos and darkness. But if you read more closely, you will recognize that the opening image of Genesis is not just darkness and void. We read clearly in Genesis 1:2 that "the Spirit of God was hovering over the waters." Even the primordial chaos had its limits. God's Spirit has always set limits as to how far the darkness can spread. There is potential in any mess. By God's hovering Spirit, there is hope and possibility even in the midst of darkness. The mess is only the beginning of the story. It's only the beginning of yours. God will not let the darkness remain for long.

When I arrived as senior pastor of my first church, I had eighteen people in the congregation and the church was a broken mess. I want to use the word *mess* as I read it in the opening of Genesis. It was darkness and chaos. Most of the people attending the church were living in deep brokenness. Their lives were dysfunctional and full of pain. Their families were broken. Their relationships were broken. Their faith was broken. There were many who had experienced multiple marriages, had lost children, and were struggling with addictions. The church did not function like a church, and most were not living the faith to which they had confessed.

We all face difficult seasons, and most churches have several members facing brokenness and chaos at any given time. Still, I had never experienced so many people trying to worship together in such a broken state. To use the language of Genesis 1:2, the church "was formless and empty, and darkness was over it." I was called to be their pastor.

I knew it would be hard work. But God had called me, and I was determined to bring the light of the gospel to that darkness. My job would be to lead them toward true faith and help them heal and change. It was going to require big commitments from all involved. They were all going to have to go on independent journeys. Their families were going to have to go on a journey. The church was on a journey, and as their pastor, so was I. I rolled up my sleeves, began to pray, and got to work. I soon found something I hadn't anticipated. I wasn't starting the work. What I found within that church of eighteen broken lives was that the work had already begun before I arrived. I began to sense how God's Spirit had been hovering over them even in the chaos and darkness. I found lives, though broken, already being worked on by the Spirit.

They could not see how God was at work; the darkness had blinded them. But I did not initiate the change. The Spirit was already there. I began to hear their stories of how in moments of utter darkness—sitting in bars, entering affairs, and beginning addictions—the Holy Spirit had spoken to them, convicted them, and drawn them back. There was work to do, but the Spirit had been hovering and preparing them for it. I felt my faith building. There was real potential. Perhaps more than I had recognized. The Spirit always sees more in our mess than we can. The Spirit is always at work before we are.

There is no darkness nor chaos so great that God's presence is denied. Over the waters of chaos, the Spirit hovered, and over the chaos of our broken lives, His Spirit continues to work. We may be in darkness, but His Spirit is restraining it. The Spirit is keeping open the possibility of new creation. The Spirit is stirring. The Spirit is planting. The Spirit is speaking. There is always a spiritual possibility even in the heart of darkness.

I watched as the lives of that little congregation were turned around. I watched as the Spirit gave growth and fruit to the seeds planted. I watched as addictions were broken, marriages were restored, and miracles were received. I watched as lives were restored. And I learned a lesson I will never forget: God can bring order out of any chaos. God can speak light into any darkness. No mess is beyond the possibility of His creative process.

As a pastor, I've continued to see broken people walk into my churches. I've seen them under the discouragement and weight of the mess they have created. Sometimes it is a mess. After pastoring for decades, there isn't a category of brokenness I haven't seen: depression, anxiety, addiction, lust, envy, anger. Sometimes the mess is so bad it's beyond my wisdom to fix it. But as a pastor, part of my job is helping people sense the possibilities of what the Spirit might be doing. I don't bring the Holy Spirit to them. The Holy Spirit is there preparing the work. My job is to help build their faith in what God is already doing.

God's work always begins with that hidden potential. It's in the hovering of the Spirit over the dark water. As the biblical scholar Stanley Horton put it, "In this stage of preparation with the Holy Spirit hovering over the primeval ocean, God was preparing for the fruition of creation which would take place during the following 6 days of creation."[1] It was true of creation, it is true for so many broken lives I've pastored, and it's true for whatever challenge you're facing. Right now, the Spirit is preparing you for those same stages of new creation. By His Spirit, there is potential in whatever situation you face.

I hope you sense that in your life. It doesn't matter what kind of darkness you're facing, and it doesn't matter how great the sin or brokenness; God's Spirit has been hovering over your life. He has been there in all those moments. He is hovering there now. The Spirit recognizes the opportunity to turn your mess into something better. Even as you read this, the Spirit is working in you and guiding you. Your task is to yield yourself to the potential His Spirit is speaking. Your job is to believe. Have faith. God is not done in your situation. He's just getting started.

We Make a Mess of It

It's not hard for most people to recognize the mess. We all know when life isn't working. What is hard to acknowledge is that despite our best efforts, we usually make the mess worse. We aren't good at putting things back together on our own.

Consider the first humans and the mess they made. Adam and Eve made a big mistake eating the forbidden fruit. They knowingly disobeyed God and rebelled against Him. Having eaten the fruit, they immediately sensed their own nakedness. They were overcome with shame and humiliation. They hadn't experienced that before. In one deliberate act of disobedience, they broke the garden's goodness and willfully sacrificed the order God had created for them. They unleashed chaos and quickly felt the consequences.

What was their response to this new disordered experience? They attempted to hide their nakedness by making garments for themselves from leaves, and they hid from God in the bushes. They tried to fix the problem and only managed to make a bigger mess. Once caught, Adam blamed both Eve and God. Eve blamed the serpent. They couldn't even take responsibility for what they had done.

That is human nature. We always think we can fix it. We always think we can figure out how to put the things we've broken back together. When we fail, we look for someone else to blame. But as Adam and Eve soon found out, the process of restoration is not ours—it is God's. Adam and Eve would experience the mess they had made. They would be expelled from the garden. They would toil to grow crops from the ground. Pain would come with childbirth. But it would also be through Adam and Even that new creation would come. A descendent of Adam and Eve would one day crush the serpent of chaos and bring light and order back to humanity. They would have to trust God and learn to recognize His plan.

Adam and Eve were not the only humans to make things worse. Almost every character in the Bible messed up and further contributed to the mess. They also struggled to trust God and recognize His plan. Let me give you a couple of examples.

God took up the work of forming a people through Abraham. Though Abraham and his wife were too old to have a child, God promised them a son and that their descendants would be as numerous as the stars. Abraham and his wife grew impatient. They felt the time was running out. They felt the darkening pressure of their own desperation. They formed a plan for Abraham to produce a child with Hagar, their servant. That had not been God's plan, and it turned their lives into a mess. Hagar gave birth to a son, and immediately there was conflict in their home. The conflict played out for centuries through their descendants. Abraham was like us. Impatient and struggling to trust God's process, he attempted to take matters into his own hands and made a bigger mess.

Or consider the life of Moses. Even having been raised in the house of Pharoah, Moses identified with his own people, the Hebrews, who were trapped in Egyptian slavery. Moses must have felt some divine calling to lead his people to freedom. He would eventually accomplish that goal, but he first attempted to do it in his own timing and by his own process. Moses struck down an Egyptian taskmaster, hoping the Hebrews would rally behind him. They didn't. In fact, the slaves he rescued turned on him and began to mock him. It was another mess. Moses had to abandon his home and people. He was forced to flee into the wilderness.

Both men had a sense of God's promises and the stirring of His Spirit. But both struggled to accept the process. Both grew impatient and tried to work their own plan.

Both ended up with a bigger mess. Our plans don't usually work out as we imagine them. As the book of Proverbs explains, "Many are the plans in a person's heart, but it is the LORD's purpose that prevails" (19:21).

I'm sure you could make your own list of failures and how your best efforts failed. We all have stories of messing up and making things worse. It's important to remember that chaos and darkness are not just one-time experiences. Christians have long recognized we face many seasons of darkness. We face times of distance and chaos and confusion.

Perhaps you find yourself in a midlife crisis moment. Maybe you've received difficult news or made a terrible mistake. You could be in an unexpected season of doubt. Even after serving the Lord for years, it's possible to face new uncertainties. It's easy to feel as if you've moved backward. Progress you thought you'd made feels lost. It's easy to get discouraged.

Too often, our failures can lead us to give up on God. We grow frustrated, bitter, and then give up. Our faith fails. We accept the brokenness and darkness as just how life is. Perhaps you are in a moment in which you're considering giving up, too. Perhaps there is a situation in which you are struggling to keep believing. Recognize that situation, but also recognize that it's in those places of darkness God speaks light. Every new season of confusion is an opportunity for new revelation. By God's process, there is always potential. Perhaps this book is just what you need to believe again and to recognize the work God wants to do in you.

God works the same process over and over in your life. That's how He brings about growth. Change often requires repetition. What holds us back is not new challenges. What holds us back is misunderstanding God's process and fighting against it. The more you learn how God works through process, the more you can engage with what He is doing and receive the change He's working in you.

I've seen plenty of messes, and I've seen just as many people make the situation worse with their own plans and schemes. I've seen people stuck, unwilling to trust God's process. Your situation isn't as unique as you might think. None of us has what it takes to solve our own problems. Our deepest needs are not things we can fix. It's true of our lives as individuals, but it's also true of our homes, churches, and nation. The things we face cannot be solved with a better plan or a new strategy. For real change, there is only one source. Real life change happens only through the power of the Holy Spirit and the creative process of God. We must learn it and trust it in each new challenge.

The Spirit and the Seed

The Bible often refers to the work of God as a seed. It was one of Jesus' favorite images. A seed is an image of potential. How remarkable that the largest tree grows from a seed small enough to be crushed by your fingers. No one is impressed by a seed. No one pays much attention. A seed on the ground is easily lost. But that seed, small, vulnerable, and often overlooked, contains the potential to become a tree that is unbreakable and unmovable by the strongest storms and winds. A seed can grow into a plant that will produce thousands of more seeds. It spreads and can eventually cover a field. From one seed comes an astonishing harvest. The next time you see a seed, take a moment to recognize its potential. Others may not see it, but you're learning to recognize things that can only come about through a process. You're learning to recognize the value of a process. Jesus suggested you see your own life in that seed.

Before a seed can mature and reproduce, it must go through a process. There are many dangers and threats that can rob it of its progress. Jesus made that point as well. He explained to the crowd:

> "A farmer went out to sow his seed. As he was scattering the seed, some fell along the path, and the birds came and ate it up. Some fell on rocky places, where it did not have much soil. It sprang up quickly, because the soil was shallow. But when the sun came up, the plants were scorched, and they withered because they had no roots. Other seed fell among thorns, which grew up and choked the plants. Still other seed fell on good soil, where it produced a crop—a hundred, sixty or thirty times what was sown."
>
> Matthew 13:3–8

The process of growth requires good seed in good soil. But before the seed can grow, it must be pressed down into the darkness of the soil. The seed must begin in the ground. It begins to grow beneath the surface. The soil is a place of decay and darkness. But the seed does not die. Life hovers over it, and its potential begins to break through. If the seed is not pressed down, the birds will steal it. If it is not pressed down deep enough, it will be scorched. The seed needs to be pressed down into the darkness of good soil to grow. It's in the darkness that it begins to grow.

Jesus' disciples did not understand the parable. They later came to Jesus and asked Him to explain it. Jesus told them, "The seed falling on good soil refers to someone who hears the word and understands it. This is the one who produces a crop, yielding a hundred, sixty or thirty times what was sown" (Matthew 13:23). By comparison, Jesus explained that the other seeds were lost. For some, the evil one snatches away the seed. Others believe, but during trouble or persecution, they give up and the process is cut short. Some find their faith choked out by the worries of this world. In each case, God's process is abandoned.

The only seed that lasts is that seed pressed into good soil, those who hear and understand. What do those hearers understand? They understand that they need God's Spirit to rework their lives. They need to submit themselves to Christ and His process of sanctification. They need the right ground in which to grow. That depends on the Sower.

Those who hear and understand are willing to submit their lives to God's process. That begins even when our lives are a mess. It begins even when things look chaotic and dark. It begins even when we don't see a path toward something better. It begins when the Sower casts that seed on good ground. We are each called to die to ourselves. We are called to lay down our lives, plans, expectations, and timelines. We are called to be buried with Christ so that, like that seed pressed down into the dark soil, we might be raised with Christ to new life.

———

If you are facing a mess, either one of your own making or one you've inherited from someone else, I want you to know there is hope. There is always hope. God has sown good seed in your life, and it is growing, perhaps ready to break through the soil at any moment. God's Spirit is at work in you and hovering over your situation. Your life has potential. Your situation has potential. This is not the end of your story; it's only the beginning of what God wants to do in you. But it will require you to surrender your mess to Him.

You will not be able to fix it on your own. The more you try, the bigger the mess will be. You can't buy your way out of it. You can't put it back together. You can't construct a plan that will fix it. You can't avoid it, either. You need what only God can do. You need His power of creation to work a new process in you. He's ready to do that.

Right now, would you be willing to be honest with Him? Pray to Him. Describe the situation you're facing. Acknowledge the darkness you're experiencing. Acknowledge the role you've played in it. Ask for His forgiveness and place your mess in His hands. Step into His process. Commit to walking with Him through it. Recognize that you are in that opening scene of creation. Your situation is formless, chaotic, empty, and dark, but His Spirit hovers over you. Do not lose hope. God is just getting started.

This is the moment just before He speaks light into your darkness.

"For I know the plans I have for you," declares the LORD, "plans to prosper you and not to harm you, plans to give you hope and a future."

Jeremiah 29:11

3

PHASE 1

Revelation

And God said, "Let there be light," and there was light. God saw that the light was good, and he separated the light from the darkness. God called the light "day," and the darkness he called "night." And there was evening, and there was morning—the first day.

—Genesis 1:3–5

Into the chaos of darkness, God spoke light. "Let there be light," He commanded. And there was. God saw that it was good. It was good because light changes things. Genesis tells us that the light pushed back the darkness. In His first creative act, God separated the light from the dark. He created day and night and marked His first act of creation as the first day. Light is how God's creative process begins. It is a powerful image, light bursting through the darkness as the power of God's spoken word began to give form to the chaos, but it also raises a question.

When we think of the light, we think of the sun. It is the sun and moon that move each day into the periods of day and night. But according to Genesis, God did not create the sun, moon, and stars until day four. So, what was that initial light that marked day one and the beginning of God's process? The light of day one was not just a chemical reaction of gases burning in the sun. The light of day one was something supernatural.

Do you remember the final image of the book of Revelation? A city is described descending from heaven. It is a place of God's perfect design, free of sin, pain, and loss. In Revelation 21 we read, "The city does not need the sun or the moon to shine on it, for the glory of God gives it light, and the Lamb is its lamp. The nations will walk by its light, and the kings of the earth will bring their splendor into it" (vv. 23–24). Revelation is describing that same supernatural light, God's presence, having finally dispelled all darkness for eternity. In that final city, there will be no need for a sun, for God's very presence will flood the streets with perfect light.

That light, emerging by God's word in Genesis 1, is not just a lesson in science, it is a lesson in the creative process of God and a spiritual principle of God's work. Every new work begins with light. Every change worked by the power of God begins with a revelation. It begins with the pushing back of darkens to reveal what is and what can be.

Scripture is filled with stories of the spiritual war against darkness. We've also personally experienced the battle and seen the consequences of that darkness. It blinds us. It distorts our view of our own lives. It keeps us from recognizing the potential of what God can do in the mess of our situation. David recognized this in Psalm 107:10 when he wrote, "Some sat in darkness, in utter darkness, prisoners suffering in iron chains." The prophet Isaiah warned, "Woe to those who go to great depths to hide their plans from the LORD, who do their work in darkness and think, 'Who sees us? Who will know?'" (Isaiah 29:15). John recognized that some even come to love the darkness. How many choose to stay in their chaos? We choose darkness because we become accustomed to it.

Make no mistake, there is a spiritual war going on, even in your situation. But God is not content to let the darkness overwhelm you. He will not let the darkness win. In his commentary on Genesis, Dr. Blackaby writes, "The initial light can best be described as an enemy of darkness."[1] God begins by pushing back the darkness that hides our sins and distorts our view of what is possible. Though Isaiah warned of the consequences of darkness, he also recognized that God was willing to lead us out of it. God was willing to confront the darkness. Isaiah wrote, "I will lead the blind by ways they have not known, along unfamiliar paths I will guide them; I will turn the darkness into light before them and make the rough places smooth" (42:16).

Where there is light, there cannot be darkness. That is one of the oldest and most foundational truths of God's creation. It is true of the physical world, but it is also a spiritual reality. God separates light and darkness. When God speaks light, the darkness is forced to retreat. Light has power over darkness. God's first word was His commitment to lead us out of darkness. God will not abandon you to the chaos. He will not leave you in your mess. God's first creative act is to shine light into every place of your darkness to dispel it. God's desire is to bring light into your situation regardless of how dark it seems.

Have you ever noticed how often Jesus healed the blind? All four Gospels include stories of Jesus healing the blind. Jesus also talked a lot about spiritual blindness. Certainly, Jesus was healing those who needed a physical touch, but His emphasis on blindness also draws our attention to a spiritual reality. Bartimaeus called out to Jesus from the crowd. Jesus asked what he desired. Bartimaeus answered, "Rabbi, I want to see." Immediately, Bartimaeus received sight and followed Jesus along the road. At Bethsaida, Jesus placed spit on a blind man's eyes. "Do you see anything?" Jesus asked him. He answered, "I see people; they look like trees walking around." Jesus again placed His hands on the man's eyes. His eyes were opened, and he was fully healed. He saw with perfectly clarity. (See Mark 8:24, 10:51.)

Before the apostle Paul was a Christian missionary and evangelist, he was a persecutor of Christians. Saul, as he was called in the book of Acts, was on his way to Damascus to arrest believers. But on that road, Saul had a divine encounter with the risen Christ. Seeing Jesus blinded him. For three days, Saul could not see. He had not been physically blind before, but those days of darkness were a divine judgment on the spiritual blindness in which he had been living. On the third day, Jesus sent one of His followers, a man named Ananias, to pray for Saul. Placing his hands on him, Ananias explained he had been sent so that Saul might see again and be filled with the Holy Spirit. Immediately, scales fell off Saul's eyes. He could see, and he was forever changed. It's significant that the incredible ministry of the apostle Paul began with a lesson on vision.

Saul not only received his physical sight, but he received a revelation and a new reality. Saul saw everything in a new light. He had seen Jesus, and because of that light, his entire situation had changed. He was on a new path and beginning a process of being re-created. He would no longer be a persecutor of Christ. Because of a new revelation, because the light came on, he would now be Christ's servant and apostle.

Do not underestimate the power of a revelation from God. When God shines His light into your situation, when you are given spiritual vision to see your situation with new clarity, everything can be changed in a moment. I was not raised by the Jewish Sanhedrin as Paul was, nor in a home of darkness and sin. I was raised in a good, Christian home. I saw the world through the reflected light of my parents. They were my lamps, and they read to me and taught me from the Bible, which is a light to our path. But that light, as helpful as it was, could not replace my own moments of God needing to personally say to me, "Let there be light."

One of those times came when I was still in college. I was working an evening shift loading trailers with freight to be delivered the next day. As I left home for work one evening, my father asked me if I had heard anything from God about a call into pastoral ministry. I said, "No. I am called to be a good church member, not a pastor!" That night as I was working, I felt the world become darker and heavier. It seemed as if the Lord was leaving me. Within a few moments, the darkness became unbearable. I knelt down on the freight and prayed, "God, are You are calling me into full-time ministry and away from business? Is the darkness and heaviness because I am not submitting to that call? I submit to Your call. I say yes." That moment, the world became bright again and the heaviness left. To me it was a "Let there be light" moment.

When God says, "Let there be light" and the darkness retreats, your whole life can be changed. That is what you need more than anything else. You need new revelation. You need a word from God, a divine light, and a new vision for what is and what can be.

What Light Does

Light is revelation. It's important we take a moment to think about what revelation is and what it does. This first stage of God's creative process allows us to see things as they are. Light may not physically change anything, but it does allow us to see what is already there. Light can entirely change our perspective on a situation. Light reveals things. There can be no real change without first having a clear view of where we are and the path before us.

My wife likes to decorate and likes to rearrange the furniture in our house. It's an easy way to make a space feel new. She'll move the couch to the other side of the room and turn the chairs in a new direction. The end table moves from one corner to the other, and the coffee table gets turned ninety degrees. It happens frequently enough that my brain doesn't always remember it. Getting up in the middle of the night, I'll move through the room, still half asleep and in the dark. I only remember the change when my shin slams into the newly positioned coffee table or I trip over that chair now placed in what was once was a clear path.

If I was smart, I would turn on the light. The light wouldn't move any obstacle out of my way, but it would help me see what was in front of me. That's how light and revelation work. Without light, we stumble over every obstacle. Without light, we constantly trip and fall. Many of us live that way. We walk around in the dark taking baby steps with our hands flailing in front of us trying not to run into things we can't see. We move based on what we remember, what we have seen in the past, or where we have tripped before. That's no way to make real progress. That's not how God intends for us to live and move in this world.

What God wants to give us is vision. You probably remember Proverbs 29:18 (KJV): "Where there is no vision, the people perish." The New International Version translates it, "Where there is no revelation, people cast off restraint." Proverbs isn't talking about a church vision statement or some abstract hope for the future. Proverbs is describing a spiritual vision for everyday life. When we live in darkness, the best we can hope for is stumbling. When we cannot see, we cannot make progress. Where there is no revelation, where there is no light, people will perish in darkness.

Your vision depends on having light. That's how the human eye works. Light is what allows us to see, and our eyes are astonishingly good at seeing light. Scientists say that on a completely clear, dark night, the human eye can theoretically see a single candle flame flickering at 1.6 miles away.[2] It doesn't take much. You are optimized to see even the smallest light. But it's more than that. Light is how we see the entire world. Your eyes have been perfectly designed to capture light and convert it into an image of the world around you. Without light, you couldn't see at all. Without light, we would all be blind.

Unfortunately, we sometimes don't recognize how much our vision is failing. We don't realize how dim our world has become. Often people who receive new glasses or contacts are surprised by how much clarity they had been missing. Having spent years in dim or blurry vision, new glasses suddenly brighten the world and add astonishing new details and color.

As I've grown older, I've come to realize how important light is. When the light is dim, I struggle to see. In a dark restaurant or at night, I have trouble reading small print. The problem is always solved by turning up the light. The more light, the easier it is to see, even when the print is small. Sometimes you don't realize how much trouble you're having until the light comes on. Once things become clear, once your eyes adjust, you quickly realize how little you were seeing. You've been squinting and straining to make out what is suddenly clear.

That experience is true for how many of us live spiritually. We squint and strain and stumble our way through life. The world and the future in front of us feels dark and blurry. We move slowly. Sometimes spooked, we rush forward in the darkness, but very rarely do we see clearly where we are or where we're going. We get used to it. We think that's just all there is to see. But by God's grace, when He flips the light on, we suddenly see with perfect clarity the mess we have been living in.

That is how God always begins to bring about change. God speaks light into existence and pushes back the darkness that blinds us. Let there be light is a command of revelation; it is an act of vision. It begins God's process of working change in your life and situation.

How Much Light Do You See

Light is an important part of an eye exam. Optometrists typically take patients into a dark room and shine a bright light into their eyes. Sometimes, eye doctors will dilate the eyes of their patients to allow more light into the lens. As with our physical eyes, we also need to take time to check our spiritual vision. How clearly can we see what God is doing? How much of His light is at work in our lives? How much have we grown accustomed to the darkness?

One day, in the perfect light of God's heavenly presence, we will see and understand all things with perfect clarity. For now, as the apostle Paul explained, "we see through a glass, darkly" (1 Corinthians 13:12 KJV). For now, we see some things only in part. But that can never become an excuse to ignore the things God is trying to show us. My experience as a college student was that God was willing to show me more than I was willing or wanted to see. God is often ready to reveal new things to us. We're the ones who choose to keep living in darkness.

That is one of the challenges faced when encouraging people to receive God's work in their lives. Often people don't think they need it. People don't realize how poorly they see their own lives. It's often easier to see brokenness in the lives of others than it is to see it in our own lives. We think we are living with wisdom. We think we're doing the best we can. We sometimes think the way we are living is the only way of doing life. We can't see our own brokenness. Being dysfunctional and recognizing our dysfunction are two completely different things. Sometimes the places where we are the most dysfunctional are the places in which we struggle the most to see clearly.

It's worth asking if there might be places like that in your life. Are there places you've quit looking at? Are there behaviors and actions you've never questioned? Are there places of dysfunction you've just accepted as the way you are? Seeing those parts of your life in a new light is not always easy. God's light exposes things as they really are. When God shines His light into your life, He is often revealing sin. Go into that old, abandoned house at night and flick on a light and you'll see all the rodents and insects scrambling for cover. They are threatened by light. It's no different when the light goes on in our own lives. Sin in the darkness of our hearts does not want to be seen.

The sin in us recoils at being exposed. The light initiates a struggle. Often, we want the darkness back. We find ourselves discouraged and embarrassed by what we see.

There is a temptation to go back to ignoring it. There's a temptation to love the darkness because it allows us to hide what we don't want seen.

God is working to change us and lead us into a better life, but we can reject God's creative process by refusing light and choosing darkness. We cannot move forward without light to guide us. We cannot change without seeing what needs to change. God cannot work His creative process in us or in our current situation without us seeing it for what it actually is. That kind of change requires revelation. We will not do it on our own. We can't. We're too blind to it. On our own, we will continue to cover it up. We will justify it and cling to the darkness. Until we see clearly, we will not change.

But do not be discouraged. The first revelation of God's light may be our need, but there is a second revelation that comes with it. God will never show us a disfunction in our life without also showing us His power to change it. The light may reveal our broken situation, but it also reveals God's power to create change. Light not only reveals what was hidden, light reveals itself. Light reveals the power of God over all darkness.

That is one of the great truths of Scripture. God reveals Himself to us. We do not seek God. We do not seek light. No one understands God or obeys Him on their own. But God does not leave us to wallow in the darkness of our mess. God takes the initiative. God speaks. God reveals. God breaks through the darkness with the light of His presence. The light of God's truth, as convicting as it may be, is never for our condemnation. God reveals Himself and our need so that He might work in us. Light is the beginning of the process. It's light that begins our healing and illuminates a path forward.

Perhaps no one has described it as powerfully as John in recognizing the revelation of God in the birth of Jesus. John writes, "In him was life, and that life was the light of all mankind. The light shines in the darkness, and the darkness has not overcome it. . . . The true light that gives light to everyone was coming into the world" (1:4, 9).

The Light of Our Path

Let me give you an example of vision from the life of David. When David arrived on the scene and heard the giant Goliath mocking the God of Israel, he couldn't understand why no one had done anything about it. David was new to the scene. Unlike his brothers, he hadn't spent the last forty days listening to Goliath's taunts. David heard and saw the situation in a different light. He was walking in a different revelation than they were.

David had been alone with God, seeking His face and worshiping Him while watching the family's flock of sheep. He had seen how God gave him strength over a bear and a lion. His revelation of God and of giants was different than every one of the soldiers hiding behind their rocks. God had revealed Himself to David, and it was that revelation that allowed David to step up when all others stood paralyzed. David marched out alone and without training or the proper weapons to fight an enemy twice his size. It was not David's natural ability but his revelation of God that allowed him to do what no one else would.

When your revelation is determined by the words and attitudes of those around you, you share in their chaos and mess. You will find yourself paralyzed by the same fear that paralyzes everyone else. Most Christians borrow their revelation. Most only know the words of the world. They listen to the opinion of others and adopt them as their own. They evaluate every situation by the power of this world and its limitations. That is not how God wants His people to live. He offers us revelation for something greater than this world. Understand that your revelation is a lid to everything in your life. God wants to give you a new revelation so that He can do new things in your life.

Vision allows us to see things we couldn't see before. Vision allows us to see distance. We can see not only what things are but what they could be in the future. It is in that space that God gets to be God.

Before God can work the needed miracle, you must "stretch your tent curtains wide . . . lengthen your cords, strengthen your stakes" (Isaiah 54:2). We must learn to see more light than we're accustomed to. We must make room for it even though it will expose our inefficiencies and dysfunctions. When the people of Jerusalem agreed with Nehemiah and accepted his dream of a rebuilt wall, they were admitting that they had allowed it to go unrepaired for decades. But once they saw what Nehemiah revealed, they found a new unity and purpose.

For those who accept the light of His revelation, their vision becomes their purpose. Vision and purpose combine into inspiration. God's light gives hope to every situation. Though the Bible often speaks of the blindness of our spiritual eyes, it continually testifies to the hope we have of our vision being restored by God.

After His resurrection, Jesus appeared to two of His followers walking home on the road to Emmaus. Though they had followed Jesus and had great expectations about His ministry, they were grieved by His death and were surprisingly unable to recognize Him as He joined them, alive, on the road. It was as if their dashed expectations blinded them. They had not understood who Jesus really was or what He had done. The revelation was not clear to them.

But as they sat and began to break bread with Him, "Their eyes were opened and they recognized him" (Luke 24:31). The two men said to each other, "Were not our hearts burning within us while he talked with us on the road and opened the Scriptures to us?" (v. 32). Suddenly they could see. They saw not only the identity of Jesus, but they saw their lives and paths changed by His presence. They had seen His light, and by it, they saw a new purpose for their lives. The two men got up from the table and rushed back to Jerusalem to tell the other followers what they had seen.

It's all there in that story. You can see the discouragement of their blindness. You can see the hopeless feeling of their situation. You can also see how Jesus came and revealed Himself, giving the men vision. They were not ashamed of their mistake; instead, they were filled with a new hope and purpose. They turned and found the path before them clear.

The Bible repeatedly echoes this same effect of revelation. David prayed, "Open my eyes that I may see wonderful things in your law" (Psalm 119:18). Paul wrote to the Ephesians, "I pray that the eyes of your heart may be enlightened in order that you may know the hope to which he has called you" (Ephesians 1:18). And we can't forget the psalmist's description: "Your word is a lamp for my feet, a light on my path" (Psalm 119:105).

When revelation comes, the light always does three things. First, it reveals our need. It exposes sin and dysfunction. Second, it reminds us of God's power. He is greater than darkness. He has come into the world to work a new creation. Third, it gives us a path forward to greater purpose. We are given hope. His light will guide you. He is beginning a new work. Light is always the first step of His creative process.

What you must be willing to do is pray as all those witnesses of Christ suggest. Pray for God's light. Pray that He opens your eyes. Pray that you might be enlightened and that your situation might be made clear. Fight the temptation to accept things as they are or to remain in darkness. Pray as David did: "Open my eyes" (Psalm 119:18).

Just as the amount of light your eyes can see is a lid to your physical vision, the amount of God's revelation in your life is the lid to what God can do in you. Your spiritual life depends on light. You may have settled for that past momentary burst of light that led you to faith and allowed you to see enough to say yes. Yet too many live the rest of their lives by that single moment of revelation.

God longs to do far more than that in you. What you need is not one moment of revelation—you need a growing light. You need new revelation. You need a path leading you toward that ever-increasing light of truth. You need eyes and a heart pursuing more truth, more light, more change. You need eyes that are not growing dimmer but that are growing clearer.

Perhaps you have been praying over a difficult or painful situation in your life. Perhaps you think you know exactly what you need and how your life could be fixed. But maybe you don't see your life or your situation with the clarity you actually need. What you need first is not just a fix for your situation; what you need is light. You need a new revelation from God. You need clarity of vision.

That is exactly where God wants to begin working change in your life. That is where God's creative process always begins. The sooner you can see what He wants to show you, the sooner His creative process can continue unfolding in your life.

Day one is the light of His revelation. But day two is also coming. God is not done. His revelation is just the beginning.

> Do not gloat over me, my enemy! Though I have fallen, I will rise. Though I sit in darkness, the LORD will be my light.
>
> Micah 7:8

PHASE 2

Atmosphere

And God said, "Let there be a vault between the waters to separate water from water." So God made the vault and separated the water under the vault from the water above it. And it was so. God called the vault "sky."

—Genesis 1:6–8

On the second day of creation, God separated the waters above from the waters below. God created space, and He called that space *sky*. Some translations refer to it as a vast expanse. What had been chaotic water, revealed by the light of His first day's work, now took on space. Do not mistake space for emptiness. The expanse God created was the atmosphere that would be needed for the rest of God's creative process. He continued His work by creating atmosphere.

But the atmosphere often appears invisible to us. We can't see it, and rarely do we pay attention to it. We cannot see the air we breathe, but it fills our lungs and sustains all of life. It is critical but invisible. It usually takes a change in the atmosphere for us to recognize that it is even there. Fill the air with the smoke of wildfires and we recognize it. Climb a mountain and we quickly realize the air is thinner.

It's true spiritually, as well. The unseen world has an impact on things that more naturally attract our attention. The atmosphere is critical, but without careful attention, we might miss its pivotal place in God's creative process.

As a creator, God not only concerned Himself with the visible forms of His creation, but He also intentionally created the space, the atmosphere, for His creation to grow and thrive. Part of His creative process was establishing the necessary conditions for life. It's hard to imagine what that second day of creation might have looked like. Would there have been any discernable change? As we said, atmosphere can be hard to see. The vast expanse and the gases that filled it are not things we often think about. Unable to see it, we neglect it. So, we read past that critical stage of God's process without recognizing how important atmosphere is. We often fail to see its significance in the creation of the universe, as we often fail to see the significance of others in our lives.

A change in atmosphere is always a part of God's creative process. Wherever He seeks to create new things or grow existing things, He must first establish the right atmosphere. Life and growth depend on it. God not only recognized the necessity of atmosphere, but He called it good. Perhaps the change you've been praying for depends on that unseen work of a new atmosphere God is wanting to do in your life. We must understand that the atmosphere around us predetermines what lives and what dies.

––––––

I remember sitting in the sanctuary praying for our church. We had been growing, but I sensed God wanted to do more. I wanted Him to do more. God had given me a vision for our church and the city, but the fulfillment of that vision seemed distant. Things were not happening as quickly as I wanted. So, I prayed. I called out to God and pleaded for Him to do a new work. I asked Him to change things. I asked Him to bring about the vision. After all, hadn't He given it to me?

As I prayed and interceded for our church, I began to hear God speaking. He didn't say what I expected. Instead, God asked me, *If I gave you what you are asking, what do you think would happen?* I waited and listened, knowing there was more. He went on. *If I answered your prayers, you would not be able to sustain the changes. You and the church are not ready for what I want to do. You must change before I can answer your prayer.* Immediately, I knew that God was right. The issue was not His unwillingness to act. The issue was the change that needed to take place in us. It had nothing to do with God's ability to do what He had promised, but rather, He knew that we couldn't handle what He wanted to give us. We didn't have an atmosphere that could sustain the life He wanted to create. If we wanted to see God's promises fulfilled, we would need a new atmosphere in which to receive them.

There was an atmosphere in our church, and in me as the leader, that first needed to change. The unseen dreams, attitudes, thoughts, and values of our church had brought us only so far, but they couldn't take us any further. We could continue to produce what we were already producing, but all the work would be in vain if the atmosphere could not support it. If we wanted something new from God, if we wanted to sustain and keep alive what God would give, we would have to create a different space in which to receive it. We weren't moving through God's creative process. We were standing on chaotic waters and expecting God to fill us with fullness and life. If He had, none of it could have survived. We needed to trust His process. We needed a new atmosphere.

God is patient, and sometimes He doesn't give us what we ask because He knows we can't fully receive it. What good is it for God to act when we aren't able to fully receive? We'll watch His blessings slip between our fingers. If God answered your prayers but nothing in you changed, would you truly benefit? Would you not be right back where you started? Would your life not naturally produce the same circumstances that created your need in the first place? How many have received things from God only to have lost them and become more discouraged?

God, instead, takes the time to work His creative process. He takes the time to change the atmosphere of our lives. Part of God's creative process is forming us into the kind of people who can fully receive from Him. Our ability to receive from God and sustain the life He gives depends entirely on the atmosphere of our lives and our churches.

The significance of the atmosphere is as true for our spiritual lives as it is for the physical world around us. Maybe you've never realized how valuable our atmosphere actually is. Earth is covered by a thin layer of atmosphere, and for good reason. Scientists have described the earth's atmosphere as a safety blanket that makes life possible.[1] Most obviously, it provides the oxygen we need to breathe. Without it, we would be subjected to the empty vacuum of space.

But our atmosphere is more than just air. The atmosphere helps shield us from dangerous radiation produced by the sun. It also helps insulate the earth, allowing for moderate temperatures. The atmosphere helps circulate fresh water, drawing it up from the oceans and casting it down as rain on our fields and lakes.

Did you know that without an atmosphere, there would be no sound? In space, hearing isn't possible. Sound travels through the vibration of molecules. Our atmosphere allows sound waves to travel and be heard. Without it, there would be no received word. Without God's creative act of forming the sky above us, we would be subjected to the extremes of outer space: extreme heat and cold, devastating radiation, and empty silence. Life would simply not be possible. You see how important an atmosphere is. Yet who wakes up and thanks the Lord for air? We take the atmosphere for granted.

Even if we recognize the importance of a physical atmosphere, we often fail to recognize the importance of the spiritual atmosphere that similarly covers and protects our lives. Since it is abstract and invisible, we think very little about the atmosphere of our lives. Just as our physical atmosphere controls what kinds of life are possible, so the atmosphere we carry determines the kind of life that is possible for us. The conditions around us and in us determine what life is like and what kind of life is possible.

Consider the spaces of your life. Your home has an atmosphere. There is a climate in your home that makes things either possible or impossible. The life in your home is largely dictated by the atmosphere of your home. It's true of the school your children attend, the church where you gather to worship, and the nation in which you work and serve. So much of what is possible depends on the atmosphere around you. Thankfully, you have a God who not only recognizes it but makes the creation of new atmospheres one of the first priorities in His creative process.

New Work Requires a New Atmosphere

Praying in the sanctuary for the growth of our church, God explained that the atmosphere is what determines what lives and dies. New life depends on the right atmosphere to sustain new growth. It's that simple. That word changed not only how I prayed, but it changed what I paid attention to. I had taken the atmosphere of our church for granted. I started recognizing the values and ideas that had shaped who we were. I started seeing the space in which we lived and worship, and I recognized how, like our physical atmosphere, it set the temperature and regulated what could grow. I also began to recognize that it was our atmosphere that was holding us back. We needed to change. To receive and keep everything God wanted to do, we would have to create a new atmosphere. It wouldn't be easy.

Moses is remembered as one of the great leaders of history. Not only did he lead the Hebrew people out of Egyptian slavery, but he led them through the wilderness and helped shape them into a new people, a nation. That's no small task. Change is hard. Moses lived it. The people constantly complained, and they often rebelled against Moses. They turned to idols and abandoned God. They even pleaded, more than once, to return to Egypt and slavery. They were so difficult that God kept them in the wilderness for an entire generation. God recognized that it would take a new generation to be able to receive the full promise of the land He wanted to give them. The old generation found the new atmosphere of God's leading difficult to trust and embrace. Before they could receive the promised land, they would have to change.

What allowed Moses to stand out from his generation? What allowed him to trust and follow God? Moses had been raised and taught in a very different atmosphere. Moses was a Hebrew, but as an infant, his mother hid him in the Nile River because Pharoah had called for the execution of all Hebrew boys. Moses had a unique call on his life, and God spared him by both his mother's ingenuity and God's divine protection.

Moses was discovered in a basket amongst the reeds by the daughter of Pharoah. Moses was adopted into the house of royalty, although he was still a Hebrew, and by a courageous act, he was allowed to grow up near his mother and sister. The atmosphere that shaped the growth of Moses was the royal palace. Those conditions were very different than the conditions of his people who were living in Egyptian captivity.

Moses studied war and leadership, science and administration. He learned the conditions in which civilizations were built. He was given one of the best educations in the ancient world, and he became a great leader. Who could have imagined that this environment was preparation for him to lead his people to freedom? Even in the days of his youth, God was preparing him. God had placed him in an atmosphere that would shape him into the kind of leader God could use to lead His stiff-necked people.

But the palace alone was not enough to fully prepare Moses. Moses needed to experience his own wilderness. God changed Moses' atmosphere again. For forty years, Moses lived in the barren wilderness as a shepherd. God taught him how to survive in the same desert his people would one day pass through. Before Moses could lead God's people, God trained him in the atmosphere of leadership and wilderness.

Each change, as frustrating and confusing as it must have been for Moses, was a critical part of the creative process God was working in Moses' life. God used those very different atmospheres to shape Moses as a leader. Many of God's leaders were shaped by unique atmospheres. It wasn't just Moses. Think of Nehemiah who was prepared to rebuild Jerusalem, having served in the courts of Persia. Joseph was prepared in both Potiphar's house and in prison for the influence he would one day hold in Egypt. David learned to trust God facing bears and lions in the field as preparation for standing against Goliath before armies. Often, it was a new atmosphere that prepared God's people for God's next work. It doesn't mean those changes were easy or that they always made sense to God's people who were living through them.

The way in which God creatively changes the atmosphere of your life can feel just as disorienting as it must have to Moses and all of God's people. Without careful spiritual discernment, you can miss how God is bringing change for your good. If you misunderstand the role of atmosphere, you can end up misunderstanding the very heart of God.

Imagine a local businessman who spent most of his life working for a company he loved and hoped to retire from, until he was unexpectedly laid off. We could understand his disappointment and why he might feel like a failure. Having spent those years praying for advancement and greater influence, he must feel as if God failed him. But what if God was at work in ways he couldn't yet discern? What if God was working a process in his life to bring about an even greater calling and influence? What if God was answering the very prayers the man had for so long prayed?

To answer this man's prayers, God knew the atmosphere would have to change. Our businessman was becoming a product of the place he worked. He was being shaped by that atmosphere, and God could only answer the man's prayers by changing the atmosphere of his life. Often God's first movements of grace can feel like a threat to our status quo. But, as the Bible wisely reminds us, what others mean for evil, God can mean for good (see Genesis 50:20). Perhaps his firing finally freed him to start his own business or to land an even better job.

I'm sure you can imagine many more scenarios. A prodigal child whose situation seems to get worse the harder you pray. A pastor who knows he's been called to have an impact on his city but instead counts the years passing in relative obscurity. A bad diagnosis, the consequences of past sin, the pain of confession. Change is not easy. Sometimes we don't initially understand God's process. But we must remember, this is not our process. It is God's. He is the one who knows how to speak into existence a new creation. He recognizes changes that we are prone to overlook. And His creative process always includes a change in atmosphere—an atmosphere that can support what He is about to do.

What Cloud Follows You?

I wonder if you recognize the atmosphere around you now. Is this space around you one God has created and called you into, or is this space an atmosphere you've created, one that might be keeping you from all God has for you? You are in the middle of an atmosphere. There is always an atmosphere. Ask yourself, What is the atmosphere and who is creating it?

Do you remember the character Pigpen from the *Peanuts* cartoons? Pigpen was a mess, and everywhere he went, he was covered with a cloud of dirt and dust. It caused him problems, but he never seemed to notice or care. That's a good visual for the way we create an atmosphere. There is a personal climate that each of us carries around, and that cloud around us determines what kind of life is possible for us. We may not recognize it, but other people do.

You probably know people who change the atmosphere of a room when they walk in. There are people who make others feel comfortable. When someone filled with faith walks into the room, often the faith of the whole room changes. It can happen the other way, too. We all know people who suck the energy out of a room. We know people who make everyone feel discouraged and nervous. Each of us possesses an atmosphere. That atmosphere is created by the values and attitudes we carry with us.

But there are also cultural atmospheres in which we live. A culture defines values. Think of your home, church, and nation. Each culture values different things. What we value shapes our culture, and that culture creates an atmosphere. What makes things valuable, what gives them meaning, and what allows one thing to live and another to starve is the value we place on it. The culture in which we live is constantly making evaluations and telling us what is important. The culture around us is another way of thinking about the conditions of atmosphere. That cloud around us is the culture we've created or allowed to form unnoticed.

Peter Drucker, who was an author, management consultant, and educator, has been quoted as saying, "Culture eats strategy for breakfast."[2] I find this leadership principle to be true. We can have great ideas, cast impressive visions, form personal resolutions, pass laws, and make promises, but if our values don't change, nothing else will. What we value determines what is possible. The climate of our culture always wins. Another way to say it is that atmosphere controls reality. The things that live and the things that die are controlled not by our ideas but by our atmosphere. The only way to change the atmosphere is to change what we value.

The reason our best intentions, resolutions, and visions often fail is that we don't change what we value. We see what could be possible. The light of God's revelation helps us recognize the brokenness of our situation, and we see a vision of what is possible, but vision doesn't change what's possible. Wanting something doesn't create the conditions for having it. The greatest vision quickly withers under the wrong atmosphere. Our values bless and curse what can exist. We see what is possible, but we end up stuck because our values are still the same. Culture decides what lives.

So many people get frustrated trying to lead change in their organization or in their own lives because wanting isn't enough. We get frustrated with others, with ourselves, and even with God. Why aren't things happening? We've cast the vision. We keep repeating it. People seem to be in agreement. We really want the change we've imagined. But nothing has changed. We still value the same things. Values always win. The atmosphere hasn't changed, so change isn't possible.

It takes humility and discipline to turn your attention to the atmosphere. But unless you're willing to see the atmosphere change, little else can. What atmosphere are you carrying with you? What is the cloud that follows you around? What values are really creating the climate of your life? Might God be first trying to effect change there before He can bring change to the areas you most want? Until you value what God values, your unseen atmosphere will continue to undermine and hinder His will and vision for your life.

Don't be discouraged. The good news is that God is in the business of creating new atmospheres. He knows exactly what atmosphere we need for the change He wants to work. Just as God continued His creative process by establishing that vast expanse above the earth, He can also change the climate of your life. God can lead you into a new atmosphere. Everything may depend on it.

Let me offer some helpful advice on how to seek a new atmosphere.

Changing the Atmosphere of Your Life

Jesus offered His disciples this advice on prayer: "When you pray, go into your room, close the door and pray to your Father, who is unseen. Then your Father, who sees what is done in secret, will reward you" (Matthew 6:6). Why did Jesus recommend they pray in secret? I think Jesus wanted to help them change the atmosphere of their prayers. They needed to go to a new place. They needed to change the climate around them. They need to step out of the world's culture and place themselves in the atmosphere of God. Your secret place with God is a way of closing the door to the world. It's a way of closing out the world's values and cultural pressures constantly around you. Alone in prayer, shut up in that inner closet, you enter the throne room of God. You are certainly in a different atmosphere.

When Moses met with God, he often observed a cloud descending on the mountain and the tent of their meeting. That place where Moses met with God was a unique climate. That change in atmosphere allowed Moses to perceive clearly what God was speaking to him and the people. Moses left the mountain still glowing from his divine encounter. The atmosphere of God always changes the atmosphere you carry with you. You need a place like that. In the busy pressures and stress of work and life, you stand little chance of making lasting change on your own. You need a place where you can step into the presence of God and allow Him to rework your values.

Most often when the prophets encountered the presence of God, they felt themselves changed. "'Woe to me," [Isaiah] cried. "I am ruined'" (Isaiah 6:5). You can't help being changed in God's presence. It's not enough to get a word from God; you need Him give you a vision. You need a regular place to be changed in His presence. You need a secret place to sit in the atmosphere of His holiness and have your atmosphere changed. Become holy as He is holy.

That takes time, and often that change starts small. You must fan it into flame. A fire requires a spark and fuel to light, but once started, it's a steady flow of oxygen that allows it to burn hotter and hotter. A fire needs atmosphere. It needs fresh air constantly poured into it. Without new air, it will smother and die. Put yourself regularly in the atmosphere of God's throne room and that oxygen will feed the flame of change in your life. Protect that small ember and give it the air it needs.

Additionally, recognize the important role relationships play in your atmosphere. You've probably heard the adage, "Show me your friends, and I'll show you your future." We are shaped by the company we keep. The collision of two atmospheres affects both. The people around you have an impact on your life. You need wisdom to discern which relationships are improving the atmosphere of your life and which are complicating it. Some change requires that we change the people who are speaking into our lives.

You also need the power of God's Word. Don't forget that God created our atmosphere by speaking it into existence. "God said, 'Let there be a space'" (Genesis 1:6 NLT). The Word of God possesses the power to create new atmospheres. You need the Word of God in your life. You need voices who are speaking that Word to you. Surround yourself with the creative power of God's Word and ensure that the voices speaking into your life are those who know and speak the Word of God in truth.

Finally, you may need to make an intentional effort to invite Jesus into your life to change your atmosphere. God wants to change your situation. But perhaps you've kept that door shut. There may be parts of your life that you have never fully surrendered to God. There may be rooms in which Christ has never been permitted. Many people speak of change but aren't willing to submit their lives to Christ. If you want to change, and if you're willing to allow Jesus to work, He can change the atmosphere around you simply by His presence.

There's a story in the Bible in which Jesus changes an atmosphere. Luke records that when Jesus arrived at the house of Jairus, the people were already weeping and crying because Jairus's daughter was dead. Jesus had not made it in time. The atmosphere of the house was one of deep loss and grieving. Luke says the people in the house were crying loudly. Jesus emptied the house, and He told them, "Stop wailing" (Luke 8:52). He informed the crowd that the girl was only sleeping. They laughed at Him. They knew she was dead, and they had given up.

But Jesus took Peter, John, and James with Him into the house. He took the girl by the hand and told her to get up. Her spirit returned, and she stood up.

It is one of the great stories of Jesus' resurrection power, but it's also a story of how Jesus changed the atmosphere. Before Jesus raised her, He commanded the weeping to stop. Jesus intentionally changed the atmosphere of the house. Jesus commanded them to stop creating an environment that spoke only of death and defeat. They had no faith because they had created a climate of loss. Jesus sought to change that. The girl was only sleeping. Jesus took with Him men of faith. He took followers who knew His power and believed all things were possible. By Jesus' command, that house that had been filled with loss was suddenly filled with faith, and the impossible became possible. Life returned once faith controlled the atmosphere.

Everything you need is there in that story. Everything you need for your atmosphere to change is there. The presence of God. A prayer offered in faith. Friends who believe. The Word of God spoken in boldness. Scripture reminds us that where two or three are gathered, God promises to meet us (see Matthew 18:20). That's a good way to change the atmosphere. Find a few believers, gather in prayer, welcome Jesus' presence, and watch as He changes the atmosphere.

Do you remember those first believers gathered in the upper room with the door locked? They prayed, and fire fell. It sounded to them like a mighty rushing wind. The atmosphere of that room was changed. God poured His Spirit down, and Peter preached to the masses with a new-found boldness. That is how we receive all that God has for us. That is how God always works His creative process in individual lives and in His Church. By His Spirit, He creates a new space. He creates a new atmosphere. When His Spirit is in our midst, when that mighty rushing wind ushers in a new atmosphere, all things are possible.

So much of the frustration you feel about the lack of change in your work or personal life comes down to the atmosphere. You see things that are possible, but they are not possible until God is freed to change the atmosphere of your life. Allow God's Spirit to turn your attention to the internal work of change. Submit to His creative process, which always involves the difficult and invisible work of changing your values and adjusting the climate.

Right now, God may be more concerned with the atmosphere of your life than He is with your prayer request. He has good reasons to be. There are things He wants to do for you that will only be a blessing if you're willing to create the atmosphere to receive them. Once that atmosphere has been corrected, answering your prayers will be easy. Get the atmosphere right, and God can create and grow things you've yet to imagine. There are good things to come. You need the right atmosphere to receive them. Trust His creative process.

> When He utters His voice, there is a tumult of waters in the heavens, and He causes the clouds and the mist to ascend from the end of the earth; He makes lightning for the rain, and brings out the wind from His storehouses.
>
> Jeremiah 10:13 AMP

1. The atmosphere in your home—the love, encouragement, support, truth, or the anger, greed, selfishness, and tension—have more to do with the outcome of your children than your rules and their enforcement. Fix the atmosphere and you will change the result. When we put our efforts on changing behavior rather than the atmosphere that supports the behavior, we are wasting our opportunity and our strength. So, when God reveals a dysfunction by His light, don't start trying to change it by force. Develop an atmosphere that will only support what is good.

2. In the same way, it is the atmosphere in your church, business, and all other relationships that is determining the outcome. Write down the values that encourage dysfunctional behavior and stop feeding them. Start celebrating a list of better values until the culture shifts and the atmosphere begins to kill the wrong behavior and feed the healthy.

5

PHASE 3

Structure

And God said, "Let the water under the sky be gathered to one place, and let dry ground appear." And it was so. God called the dry ground "land," and the gathered waters he called "seas." And God saw that it was good.

—Genesis 1:9–10

On the third day of creation, God separated land from water. He began organizing the spaces: water, sky, and land. He pulled the water into its place and gathered ground out from it. By His command, a new structure emerged. Each space was given a name. There was land, and there were seas. It was upon this new structure that God could begin His work of populating the land with its first vegetation. New life emerged from the ground that could not have survived in the water. There were plants and trees and every kind of seed-bearing fruit. Life germinated and spread across the ground God had gathered from the water. The structure gave space for new life to emerge. On day three, God organized His creation for new life.

There comes a moment in every creative process in which a new structure must emerge for the change to continue. We've seen how God uses light to bring revelation and how a new atmosphere created space and support, but on the third day of God's creative work, the changes finally became visible. All the abstract work of vision and atmosphere took on a new physical form in the dirt and soil of the gathered ground. The way it is described in Genesis makes its physicality the emphasis. It is as if the Creator reached His hands into the murky water and drew the mud from the sea, separating, organizing, and structuring His new world into the coasts and hills of continents. Mountains, valleys, and fields emerged from the water.

The seas became clear, and the distinctive lines that divided land from water emerged as boundaries once the mud was removed from the water. As long as the elements of creation remained mixed and undifferentiated, life was not possible. But separated and organized, new life bloomed.

Life requires structure. The human body requires bones to support the life-giving organs. Life in all forms requires organization, systems, and structure. Change often means the elements and structure of our lives being reorganized. Though the change of restructuring is often challenging, it's also exciting. It's here that we finally see life growing and multiplying. By the end of the third day, the earth had taken on its characteristic image: blue seas and green ground. Forests, woods, and fields sprouted and spread across the ground. God's creative process was becoming increasingly visible. Change was breaking out everywhere.

It is no different for your life. There is a moment when the change becomes visibly real. And there comes a moment when we must begin to reorganize and restructure our life for that change to have its full effect. If we are willing to take up that hard work, our hands in the muddy soil of our lives, separating, organizing, and restructuring, then the signs of our change will be just as imminent. Change in your life will require a new structure for your life. That's the way God's creative process brings new life. You have to be willing to build a new structure.

———

Your life has a structure. It might not be the right structure for what God is trying to do, but you have a way of organizing the various parts of your life. We each have ways of organizing our time, resources, and interests. Your priorities always produce some kind of structure. Perhaps you've never thought much about it. And perhaps your structure feels more like chaos and disorder than organized, but it's still a kind of structure. The problem is that a structure can only support so much weight; it can only sustain so much life. If the structure of your life is still unorganized and chaotic, the change can't be sustained.

You've certainly seen ground where the dirt and water aren't separated. We call them swamps. They are places of rot and decay, places where life is wild and dangerous. No one builds a home or town in a swamp. It's too unpredictable, prone to flooding and rotting. But there are times when determined settlers have drained swamps and gone about reorganizing the land. A swamp can be made livable and fruitful, but it requires separating the water from the ground. It takes hard work and a new structure. Perhaps your life feels more like a swamp than a carefully ordered field. If you want to build lasting change, you're going to have to bring order to that disorder through a new structure. It's time to reorganize your life.

Our reluctance to restructure our lives is often due to comfort. We get comfortable with the structure because it's familiar. Even when it's failing us and holding us back, we feel attached to it. It's the way we have always done things. Even chaos can feel comfortable when it's all we have known. But it's also the reason we get the same results. It's the reason our lives are not changing. The life we get is the one we have the structure to support.

And even if your life is highly organized and structured, you may need a new structure to be faithful to the new things God is calling you to. My life has looked different as a pastor and as a leader in our denomination. It's not a question of how organized our lives are. The question is, do we have the right structure for where God is calling us to go? Our lives are always reorganizing because God is calling us to new and greater responsibilities. We can't get comfortable and keep changing. Never make a permanent commitment to a structure. The structure that got you where you are now will then keep you there. What was your ladder up will become your bondage to that level. Structures have a life-span!

It's true for any organization or church, just as it is for you personally. Culture produces structure that eventually limits new life and growth. We do the same things and get the same results. This can become a frustrating stage in God's process if we aren't willing to embrace the change. After all, God has shown us through revelation what needs to change and what is possible. We've come to understand how the atmosphere of our values keeps us from the faith needed to change, but it's easy for conversations about vision and values to remain abstract. We want to change. We see the change that is possible. We think about what change would be like. We may even pray earnestly for change. But there comes a time when God asks us to begin the physical work of reorganizing our lives to make that change last. We need a new structure.

When I first began to understand God's creative process, I wanted to see change in my life and in the church. It took me some time to realize how important structure is, and how hard it can be to change. Let me give you a personal example from my own prayer life.

I have always believed in prayer, and I pray often. But as I prayed for new growth, I sensed that God was asking me to restructure my approach to prayer. Prayer is prayer, right? I was praying, after all. The way I was approaching prayer had brought me a long way in my relationship with God, but my approach to prayer was only going to get me what it already had. We can do a lot of praying by just squeezing it into the free moments of life. Pray on our morning commute. Pray in the car line. Pray before we fall asleep at night. I'm for praying in any of those moments, but I sensed that God was asking me to organize a new and intentional structure to my praying. It was time to reorganize my prayer life, not because it had been wrong, but because only a new structure could produce new growth.

A new structure to prayer meant I would have to plan, categorize, and arrange my schedule and priorities to make more time for prayer. My morning routine would have to change. I'd have to go about my day from a different schedule. The process of restructuring my times of prayer also led me to begin restructuring other parts of my life and leadership.

At first, all of this new structure can feel limiting. We want new life, not new rules. We want growth, not new limitations. But those frustrations come only from being comfortable in the old system. They are the pains of growing. And here is the remarkable truth you'll quickly discover: A better structure produces more space in your life, not less. Organizing your life for the work God is doing doesn't limit your life; it expands it. You create space for God to do more.

This is the reason Jesus taught His disciples to go into a secret room and shut the door when they prayed. The shut door allowed the time and space for their prayers to be organized and focused. That shut door was a creative act of structuring their lives in a way that would produce new growth. Some people have no shut doors in their life. Their lives are in chaos. They are open to whatever rushes in. They are controlled by the next email, the next phone call, or the next person who walks through their door. There is no space for growth. They are constantly at the demand of others. They live reacting. Such an unorganized approach to life will always place a lid on what change is possible. You won't have space for the new work God is doing.

If God is working a creative process of change in your life or church, it will mean you have to restructure your life or church. You will have to reorganize your time, finances, and priorities. You will have to give up what is comfortable. You will have to try something new. You will have to lead that process of change. And you will have to be comfortable in the discomfort of change. But there is always new life on the other side. God always fills that new space with new life.

Peeling Away the Old Structure

A few years ago, I had the chance to visit a vineyard in Spain. I don't drink wine, but I was fascinated by the complexity required to grow and harvest grapes. The Spanish vineyard we visited had been in operation for over three hundred years, and it was unlike anything I had seen in the United States. Three hundred years of careful tending had produced grape vines with massive roots and trunks. The vines climbed upward through arched trellises that stretched over the open rows between the line of grapes. The arches were so tall that the workers could drive trucks under them, harvesting the massive cluster of grapes that hung down from above.

We walked under the plants staring high above at the grapes and marveling that such delicate vines could grow to that size. Our tour guide began to explain how generations of his family had shaped the plants to their current size. The process was slow and time-intensive but yielded what seemed to me like miraculous growth.

The process began generations ago. New plants were not placed on those massive trellises of today. What we saw hadn't even existed in the beginning. Instead, a new plant was wrapped carefully around a single horizontal wire. For years the vine inched its way across that single wire structure. It can take up to three years for the grapes to begin forming on the vines. Slowly they filled the single wire. If they had been allowed to stay on that single wire, their growth would have eventually been stunted. The structure was exactly what the new plants needed but would eventually limit growth.

There came a time when a new structure had to be inserted, and the vines had to be removed from the wire and placed on the new structure. The workers explained that this is a time-consuming and difficult process. The vines must be peeled away from the old structure and carefully placed on the new one. That process had played out again and again for hundreds of years. The work must be done every few years to keep the plants growing. Every few years, they must be reorganized around a new and larger structure. There is a cost to that work.

The process of peeling the vines from the structure that has for years shaped their growth is a shock to the plants. Untwisting a small vine from one of the wires can cause the vines to produce fewer grapes the following year. It can decrease their fruitfulness, but only for the short term. The new and larger structure will eventually allow the vines to grow much larger and produce a much larger yield. This future yield makes the work involved worth the cost. But the vineyard must be willing to take on the work and the loss for the future gain.

I looked up again at the massive grapes hanging over my head, vines climbing twelve feet in the air, and thought about the hundreds of years of work that had gone into sustaining that growth. I realized immediately how God's process of change was playing out in those vines over my head, just as it had in my own life. That process is what God wants to do in each of our lives. I'm sure many vineyards settle for less. I'm sure many aren't willing to do the work. Their vines will still produce fruit, but nothing like what I witnessed. That Spanish vineyard had paid the price. They earned the fruit of that labor. Their vines were still growing.

Your life is clinging to some structure. At this moment, it doesn't matter how great or small that structure may be. What matters is your willingness to do the hard work of peeling your life away from its current structure and carefully placing it on a new structure that can sustain the new growth God wants to do. Your life has greater potential. There is more God wants to work in you. But it will require you doing the hard work of restructuring and reorganizing your life. It may even feel as if it's moving your life backward. You may feel as though you're seeing less change—but don't be fooled. You are creating the space for new life, which is exactly the work God does before that new life emerges from the ground.

New Structures Lead to New Growth

The apostles who led the early Church found themselves in a process of rapid change, one God was obviously leading.

The small group of believers who gathered behind the locked door of the upper room to pray didn't have much structure. They had just witnessed their leader ascend to heaven. They had little more than His commission to go into all the world and His command to wait until the Holy Spirit had empowered them to do it. So, they gathered and prayed and waited.

They were changed. As the Spirit fell, they found themselves emboldened. Peter stepped forward and began to preach to the crowds. Luke records three thousand people were saved that day. In one day, the Church had multiplied many times over. That growth continued. Word spread and more people came to believe. The growth had to be exhilarating. The apostles were proving faithful to lead it. They preached, taught, and suffered along with the other believers. They shared everything, caring for one another and meeting to administer help. But as the Church continued to grow, the work became more complicated.

In Acts 6:1 (NLT), Luke records, "But as the believers rapidly multiplied, there were rumblings of discontent." Anyone who has led a church knows what Luke was recording. Problems were forming. Rumors were spreading. Things were spiraling. They were losing control because of the rapid growth. According to the book of Acts, the issue seems to have been a growing division between Christians who spoke Hebrew and Christians who spoke Greek. The Greek-speaking believers complained that the widows from their community were not getting their fair share of food distributions from the Church.

Whatever system the apostles had established to care for those widows was beginning to break down, and conflict was emerging. It had previously worked, but with the new growth, that old structure was failing. I think it's significant that Luke sets this story at the very moment that the Church was multiplying rapidly. The growth of the Church, a good thing, was creating a strain on their structure. There must have been a temptation for the apostles to drop whatever they were doing to sort out the problem. But that's not what they did. They recognized that the problem was not really about food and widows. The problem was that the Church's growth required a new structure. They recognized that they would have to lead change if they wanted to make room for what God was doing.

Luke writes,

> So the Twelve called a meeting of all the believers. They said, "We apostles should spend our time teaching the word of God, not running a food program. And so, brothers, select seven men who are well respected and are full of the Spirit and wisdom. We will give them this responsibility."
>
> Acts 6:2–3 NLT

So it was that the role of deacons emerged in the Church. The apostles created a new structure so that the Church could continue to grow and they could stay focused on their priorities of preaching the gospel and prayer.

That may seem like a small administrative detail, but I marvel at their wisdom and courage. And I think it's significant that Luke decided to record it in Acts. There is an important lesson he wanted us all to learn. It must have taken courage to lead that kind of change. How easy it would have been to cling to the structure Jesus had given them.

Jesus hadn't seen the need for deacons, so why did they need deacons? Twelve disciples had been good enough for Jesus. Why did they need anything new? They must have been tempted to keep things as they had been, but the apostles understood that while their message would not change, their structure could. They understood that for their message to stay the same, their structure would have to change.

The apostles understood that structure is never sacred. The structure may be comfortable, and it may have been exactly what was needed to produce growth up until the current moment, but it can only produce so much. Every structure has its limits. If they hadn't been willing to do the hard work of placing the Church on a new structure, they would have limited the potential growth of the Church. Instead, they gathered the people and took up the hard work of leading change.

Luke concludes the story with the powerful note, "So God's message continued to spread. The number of believers greatly increased in Jerusalem" (Acts 6:7 NLT). Growth and new life came to the Church because its leaders were faithful to God's process of creation. If you want new growth in your life or church, you will be required to reorganize and restructure to receive and sustain it.

A Plan to Reorganize

It's time for you to take a careful and honest look at your life or the church you lead. How long have you existed in your current structure? When was the last time you changed? Have you become too comfortable with your structure? Has it become sacred? If God has given you a vision for something new, it will mean restructuring your life or organization for that vision to be fulfilled. Are you willing to do it? Are you willing to lead change? Are you willing to peel your life away from what you know and place it on a new structure? Are you willing to take on new disciplines and new ways of doing things? I believe you can. I believe you must. I believe God has new life that only that new structure can support. So, how do you go about restructuring?

First, I will always encourage you to pray. Begin by restructuring your prayer life. I have often found that change requires a new focus on prayer. You're going to need courage, wisdom, and endurance. I know of no better place to find those things than in a structured place of prayer with your heavenly Father. Find the right structure of prayer to help you sustain change. That might be a new time alone each morning, that might be a new prayer team with your friends and supporters, or it might mean launching a new prayer service at your church. Begin by praying for God's wisdom and listening for His voice. God is leading this process. You are not looking for your own ideas, you are looking for God's next step. Prayer will give you wisdom and build your courage.

Often the way in which God seeks to reorganize your life is not what you would have organized. After all, you know how to organize what you already have. God knows how to build structures capable of sustaining the universe. I know that I want God's structure far more than my own. Sometimes God calls you to restructure in unexpected ways. Be willing to listen for His guidance. What does God show you that needs change?

Do you remember when Gideon was preparing to fight the Midianites (see Judges 7)? Gideon was organizing an army, an army he thought could win. According to the book of Judges, Gideon gathered more than thirty thousand men. But that wasn't the structure God envisioned. God began cutting what Gideon had sought to accumulate. He cut Gideon's army down to ten thousand men, then down to just three hundred. That's not the structure Gideon had envisioned taking into battle. Had Gideon been in charge, that's not the plan he would have drawn up. God knows better than we do. Three hundred men with trumpets were enough to defeat the entire Midianite army. That was God's plan.

That's the kind of plan you need—not one you've dreamed up alone on the whiteboard. You need the wisdom of God to help you discern the reorganization He is working. You need His wisdom. That means you need a new place and structure of prayer for encountering God and listening to His plan.

Second, there is also great wisdom to be learned from others. Ask others to join you in prayer and ask them to help you discern wise next steps. Finding the right guides and mentors is critical. We have a tendency to emulate structures and organizations that are far beyond our reach. We emulate where the masters are today without taking the time to learn each of the structures that led to their growth. Let me give you an example.

If I wanted to start my own vineyard, I would be tempted to book a plane ticket back to Spain. I'd want to tour that impressive vineyard again, marvel at the success of their vines, and steal some of their ideas, but that would be a mistake. They've spent three hundred years developing their vineyard. I'd have a lot of work to do before their structure would be relevant. Instead, I would do better to find a vineyard that was just a few structures ahead of me. I don't just need more advice and ideas; I need the right advice and the right ideas for the new structure I'm trying to build. Be careful who you are emulating, and make sure you're seeking wisdom about your situation and not just aspirations.

With prayer, guidance, and courage, God will reveal the work He wants you to do. He is leading this process. He will show you what needs to change. He will help you lead that change, and He will give you the strength to do it. What matters most is your willingness to say yes. You must decide to leave behind the comfort of what you have known. You must be willing to pay the price for new growth. You must decide to change. You must be willing to build new structures into your life.

Though it will require my time and energy, and others may not understand the work I'm doing, I'm always excited about this stage of the process because the change becomes real. Each new sacrifice creates space for God's new work. Life merges. Seeds long since planted break through the surface and begin to spread. New life springs from the ground.

On the third day of creation, God looked on as His earth turned green with new life. He looked on and recognized that it was good. The ground He had organized and separated from the waters gave space for life. Trust

His process, and the same will occur in your life. New structures always lead to new life. God will look down and again call that new life good. The hard work is always worth it because the structure that got you to where you are can only keep you there.

"But forget all that—it is nothing compared to what I am going to do. For I am about to do something new. See, I have already begun! Do you not see it? I will make a pathway through the wilderness. I will create rivers in the dry wasteland."

Isaiah 43:18–19 NLT

A PAUSE

"Come to me, all you who are weary and burdened, and I will give you rest. Take my yoke upon you and learn from me, for I am gentle and humble in heart, and you will find rest for your souls. For my yoke is easy and my burden is light."

—Matthew 11:28–30

We need to pause so that I can ask you an important question. Are you tired, stressed, or do you feel overwhelmed by the process God has you in?

God took just seven days to create the universe. He did so in a steady, ordered, uninterrupted plan of creation. He could do so because He was dealing with objects that could not talk back and did not have to voluntarily choose to participate. We've been looking at how God uses that same creative process to work change in our lives, but it's easy for the slow and sometimes monotonous pace of that change, which requires our cooperation to lead, to cause fatigue. In the process of becoming who God knows we can and should be, many grow weary. That weariness can cause us to abandon or short-cut the work God is doing. The kind of change God is working in your life, family, business, and church usually takes more than just seven days. All along the way, there is a temptation to grow tired. There is a temptation to lose patience. There is a temptation to quit.

In my experience, it is during the middle of the process that many people give up on what God is doing. I don't want you to do that. So, I want to take a short pause to talk about how you're doing and how you can maintain your faith and focus through this God-ordained process. Though you are coming to understand God's creative work in your life, you may still try to carry too much of the load. With each step of creation comes another test of faith. Each phase requires more trust in Him. We need a moment to pause and renew our commitment to what God is doing. We need a moment to remember this is God's process.

So far, much of the process we have looked at can be abstract. Perhaps you have felt the change, but you have not seen any real fruit from it. We've talked about God's revelation, about vision, and about the new disciplines of structure you're working into your life, but the effects of those changes are not always visible. Though you've spent hours in prayer and heard new words from God, no one else may notice the change taking place. You're halfway into God's process, and you may feel as if you have nothing tangible to show for it. It's here, in the middle of the process, that there is a great temptation to give up. There is a temptation to lose faith. There is a temptation to slip back into your previous ways of living. That is what you know and can see.

You may be tempted to give up simply because you are worn out. But maybe you are still trying to carry too much of the load. Perhaps you are still trying to lead the change rather than submit to it and support it. Your faith may not be complete. Are you really trusting God's process?

I want to say this as simply and directly as I can so that you might remember it and be encouraged by it: God's process of change should not wear you out. God's will is not to make you tired. He does not call you into a world of stress and anxiety. God's consistent process of change is meant to give you peace. He has shown you how He works so that you might trust Him in the middle of that change. He offers peace because He is working this change in you. You are called to submit to His process, but He is promising to lead that change.

Jesus made this explicitly clear, reminding His disciples that His "yoke is easy" and His "burden is light" (Matthew 11:30). The image Jesus offers is of two animals being yoked together in a team. The animals, usually oxen or horses, would be harnessed together to help pull a wagon or cart. Change can feel like that; it can feel as though you have been harnessed to some heavy load and asked to drag it forward. We often think that we must pull change into reality. But Jesus said that His yoke was not hard, it was easy. And the load we are asked to carry is not heavy but light.

I was once preaching on Jesus' yoke when an old farmer came up after the service to tell me about how he used to plow with teams of horses. They hadn't had enough money to buy two good horses and had to often settle for unevenly matched animals. He went on to explain how those old horse harnesses included an adjustment, which he called an evener. An evener is attached to the front of the horses and is used to distribute the weight of the load. The evener allows the farmer to adjust the load between the two horses. If one horse is larger and stronger than the other, the smaller horse can't be asked to pull the same weight. He will quickly wear out, and the larger horse will pull to his own side. You will end up driving the team in circles and frustrating the little horse. So, an evener could be attached to shift more of the weight to the stronger animal, allowing the two animals to pull according to their size and strength. The smaller horse should only be asked to pull the weight it is capable of pulling.

Most of us try to pull more weight than we have the strength to bear. We imagine God is asking us to pull more than He actually is. So, like that smaller horse, we rush forward with energy and conviction. We're excited and anxious to keep up. But we quickly wear out. We grow tired. We become frustrated. We fight against the load. But God knows how to distribute the weight correctly. His burden is light, and being yoked with Jesus is easy. If we are tired or worn out, we may be trying to carry too much of the process. We may be trying to carry too much of the change.

We don't contribute that much to what Jesus is doing. That's not how this team works. But it has never really been about what we can do. We don't take up this yoke to prove our strength; we take up this yoke so that we can be with Jesus. It has always been more about fellowship than effectiveness. Jesus wants to be with us. He's willing to carry the heavy load to do it. But will we let Him?

I want to use this moment to pause and shift the weight back onto Christ. This is His process. Change comes at His leading. I don't want you to grow frustrated or tired because there is so much God still wants to do. You need only trust Him. Take only the work He asks of you and allow Him to carry everything else. If you are tired, you need this moment to adjust the load. Do not attempt to carry more than God is asking. What He is asking, above all else, is that you simply trust His process. Have faith in how God works.

The truth is that God's change usually happens in seasons. It's learning to recognize those seasons that will free you from the stress and exhaustion of the need for constant work and change. Learning to understand God's seasons will build your faith and help you sustain it. It's at exactly this middle stage of God's creative process that He introduced seasons into creation. A better understanding of seasons is exactly what you need for this change to continue, for it to produce the fruit for which you are longing.

Paul wrote to encourage the Galatian believers, "Let us not become weary in doing good, for at the proper time we will reap a harvest if we do not give up" (Galatians 6:9). The older King James Version translates it, "for in due season we shall reap." The Bible's advice for those growing discouraged and weary is to recognize the importance of season and to persevere, believing a new season is coming.

7

PHASE 4

Seasons

"Let there be lights in the vault of the sky to separate the day from the night, and let them serve as signs to mark sacred times, and days and years, and let them be lights in the vault of the sky to give light on the earth."

—Genesis 1:14–15

On the fourth day of creation, God created the rhythm of seasons that we experience each year. He marked those seasons, directing the sun, moon, and stars in regular and predictable rotations. Those orbits of light have long been used by humanity not only to measure the passing of time but to mark the changing of seasons. Genesis tells us that these lights were given to serve as signs. They were placed in the sky to guide us in counting the days, years, and seasons of life.

For thousands of years, each day has been marked by the passing of the sun with its rhythmic rising and setting. Time passes steadily. But those days are not all the same. Time is not neutral. Time moves us through seasons. Time accumulates and marks the changes of the world around us. Since the beginning of humanity, we have lived counting our days and marking the change of seasons. God designed us to live in seasons. Seasons are a central part of God's creation and how He continues to work. If we ignore God's seasons, we miss the predictable patterns of His process.

It is a modern novelty that we can mostly ignore the seasons changing around us. Global shipping allows us to have our favorite foods any time of the year. Heating and cooling systems can keep our homes at a consistent temperature year-round. And while the seasons used to have a direct impact on most work, today, when we probably commute to an office, the seasons make little difference to the tasks on our to-do lists. Our technologies allow us to live without paying much attention to the seasons. We may feel the change in temperature or note the falling leaves out the window, but unless we are farmers or construction workers, our lives reflect very few of the changes taking place in the world around us. I'm not suggesting we abandon these modern conveniences, but can we at least note that we are now at risk of neglecting one of God's intentional acts of creation? Ignore the rhythm of seasons and we risk no longer living in the fullness of what God created and called good. We miss out on how God is still working.

If we are going to understand God's creative process and how He works to change our lives, we cannot ignore how He uses seasons to bring about new life. If we are going to experience all God has for us, we must learn not only to recognize these seasons but also how to make the most of each. Because here is another truth worth remembering: A new season doesn't begin simply because we decide to try something new. That's not how it works.

You were born into a season. You sit reading this book in another season. Wishing and wanting a new season won't produce one. That is the wrong way of looking at the world. God has given you these signs so that you might mark the coming and going of the seasons around you and in you. What you need most is to recognize the season you are already in, to embrace how God is using it, and to recognize how it is preparing you for seasons to come.

Perhaps no preacher has ever put it as well as Solomon did in Ecclesiastes:

> There is a time for everything,
> and a season for every activity under the heavens:
> a time to be born and a time to die,
> a time to plant and a time to uproot,
> a time to kill and a time to heal,
> a time to tear down and a time to build,
> a time to weep and a time to laugh,
> a time to mourn and a time to dance,
> a time to scatter stones and a time to gather them,
> a time to embrace and a time to refrain from
>   embracing,
> a time to search and a time to give up,
> a time to keep and a time to throw away,
> a time to tear and a time to mend,

a time to be silent and a time to speak,
a time to love and a time to hate,
a time for war and a time for peace.

Ecclesiastes 3:1–8

Ecclesiastes is known as a book of wisdom. Solomon was known as a man of wisdom. It takes wisdom to recognize when things should be done. I often find that people have good ideas but lack the wisdom to know when it's the right time for their ideas. We carry dreams and visions and grow frustrated when they are unfulfilled. We fail to recognize that often it simply isn't the right time. There is a season for everything. God has designed it that way. Consider how Solomon went on to describe God's wisdom of timing: "He has made everything beautiful in its time" (Ecclesiastes 3:11).

That is a remarkable statement of faith. Can that really be? God makes everything beautiful? It doesn't feel that way right now. There is probably plenty in your life that doesn't seem beautiful. But faith and the wisdom of God's creative process remind us that time is still passing. Seasons are still coming. God's creative work has not ceased. Everything will be beautiful at its right time. We must cultivate the faith to believe it. So much depends on understanding the season.

Scientists have often marveled at the complexity of the earth's seasons. It is the precise angle of our planet in its rotations that allows for the regular changing of the seasons. And it's the changing seasons that control the rhythms of growing and harvesting that sustain life on earth. Wind and rain, sun and snow, heat and cold, life and death—who can comprehend the intricacy of the earth's seasons? But our own lives are no simpler.

The pivotal moments of our lives are connected to an infinite number of factors beyond our awareness. The choices of distant ancestors, neighbors, rulers, and complete strangers. At any moment, there are millions of factors at work in what we perceive to be our situation. Who can understand the way God is at work in all of those details? We weren't created to comprehend this complexity. Neither can humanity understand the full complexity of creation. But God gave us signs: the waxing and waning of the moon, the shifting of the sun, and the rotation of the stars, the rhythms of planting, harvesting, and resting. They all remind us that things are changing. God is still working.

God is always at work. We can trust that this season is preparing us for a new season to come. God's seasons are dependable, repeatable changes in the atmosphere. Having already discussed the importance of atmosphere, you should see why each new atmosphere that a season brings is key to the change God is working. By His seasons, God not only gives new life, but He also sustains it and deepens it. God works through seasons.

Dependable and Repeatable

I often turn to Joseph's story to remind myself of the importance of seasons. Joseph's dream that one day his brothers would bow before him didn't seem realistic. When his brothers threw him in a pit and sold him into slavery, that dream must have seemed completely lost.

Dragged to Egypt, Joseph must have wondered if he would ever see his brothers or family again. What makes Joseph's story so great is how unexpected the coming events would be.

From Potiphar's house, to prison, to his rise to the throne room of Egypt, each season of Joseph's life proved a preparation for what awaited him. With famine spreading throughout the land, Joseph's brothers showed up in Egypt looking for help. They did not recognize Joseph, who now served as a powerful Egyptian ruler, so they bowed before him. He had changed in more than appearance. Time and experience had shaped him as well. He explained to his brothers, "You intended to harm me, but God intended it for good to accomplish what is now being done, the saving of many lives" (Genesis 50:20).

What Joseph came to see is how God had been working through all the seasons of his life, even those that must have felt like setbacks. There are seasons that often feel like setbacks or wasted time—but that is not how seasons work. Each season prepares the earth and its atmosphere for the next. Each season moves us forward in time. There are no setbacks, only seasons of preparation. God is always at work. He is doing things right now, perhaps uncomfortable and confusing, but things He has designed for this season to prepare us for the change that is coming.

Instead of fighting these seasons, what if you learned to make the most of them? What if, by faith, you received them? To do that will require you to trust God fully. You must learn to trust His creative process. Like the seasons we learn to depend on, even in the darkest part of winter, we know that eventually spring will come, and after it, summer. You can't control the seasons.

You can't control the seasons God has you in, either. But you can trust Him. You can find peace. And you can learn to recognize His presence with you in every season.

Just before Israel entered the promised land, Moses preached a sermon recorded in the book of Deuteronomy meant to encourage the people and remind them of how God would go with them. One of the central points that Moses made was to remind them of how God would use seasons in their new land. Moses explained:

> "The land you are entering to take over is not like the land of Egypt, from which you have come, where you planted your seed and irrigated it by foot as in a vegetable garden. But the land you are crossing the Jordan to take possession of is a land of mountains and valleys that drinks rain from heaven. It is a land the LORD your God cares for; the eyes of the LORD your God are continually on it from the beginning of the year to its end."
>
> Deuteronomy 11:10–12

The Hebrew people knew the customs and methods of living in Egypt. The Egyptians had created innovations that allowed them to guarantee water for their gardens. Moses remembered how in Egypt they watered their gardens with the simple movement of their feet. What he was describing was an ancient technique by which the Egyptians channeled water from the Nile. Channels were created that would carry the water from the river to all of the gardens of the land. When the gardens needed watering, a person could go down to the Nile and with their foot, kick open the gate, which allowed water to flood into these channels. The Egyptians no longer waited for rain. They controlled the flow of water by their own effort and technology.

So, Moses warned the Hebrews that it would not be that way in their new land. Theirs would be a land that was watered by rain. Since they could not control the falling of the rain, they would have to trust God for it. Their new gardens would be watered by God's provision alone. But Moses did not feel unnerved or worried by that fact. He reminded them that God had His eye on the land the whole year, even when it seemed that the water from the sky had dried up. They were to trust God in every season. The rain would come again. They would have to learn to live in the seasons of their new land.

That is a word for you today. Our world, like the Egyptians, imagines that we are in control of everything we need. We imagine we can simply open the gate and have whatever we want when we want it. We can go to the local store or order it online. But that is a lifestyle without God. In that way of living, you have only what you can produce, which isn't much. To live by faith is to enter a new land that God cares for. You will have to trust Him. You will have to trust His timing and His seasons.

Where are you living? How much of your life is about your control? Do you know how to live by faith? Do you trust God and His timing? Do you trust the wisdom of His seasons in your life? Can you allow God to make things beautiful in His time?

The Seasons

I once preached a series on the Bible's parables of seeds, planting, and harvesting. I quickly realized that many of the farmers in my congregation knew more about that topic than I did. I decided to form an advisory group to help with my research. Each week, I met with a group of farmers who helped describe the processes I was reading about in the Bible. They came in their pickup trucks with their John Deere caps and work boots, and I gleaned from their knowledge.

We spent a lot of time talking about seasons and the work that was required to take advantage of each season. A farmer does everything by the seasons. Their work makes no sense outside of seasons. How could you harvest in the spring? And it makes no sense to try to plant in the winter. Farmers know the wisdom of God's timing, and they learn to live by faith in what God provides through each season. So, each week, that group of farmers taught me to pay closer attention to the seasons, and they helped me recognize the spiritual lessons God embedded within them. I want to offer you some of what they taught me.

I think it would be helpful for you to imagine your own crop. The Bible often speaks of fruit trees, so you could imagine a young fruit tree—perhaps a fig or pear or peach tree—just outside your window. Maybe you have a whole orchard of them, a full-time job. I want you to look more closely at how the seasons affect those trees and the work that is required of you if you want to steward them well.

Spring

It is best to plant fruit trees in very early spring while they are still dormant, just as the ground begins to thaw from winter. There are few things better than planting in the spring. It is the season of new life. The world is full of optimism and new birth. Everywhere flowers are emerging and buds sprouting on trees. With the temperature beginning to rise, spring is a time of excitement. It is a season for new things.

We've all experienced those seasons in our lives. We know the excitement of seeing new things emerging around us. It might be new relationships, new ideas, new products, or just fresh energy for some new work. We quickly see the first sign of new growth. There are seasons when God gives us new ideas. There are seasons when there is fresh energy to start new initiatives. There are seasons new people show up and new vision flows from heaven.

In spring, this life comes so unexpectedly and with so little effort that it feels miraculous. Before long, your peach tree is covered with new limbs shooting up from last year's pruning, followed by being covered in flowers with fresh leaves unrolling on every limb. It's not the fruit you are hoping for, but it is a step in that direction. Because new fruit comes best on new limbs, we celebrate the new growth even before we see its fruit.

If we do not make room for the new limbs, new ideas, new people, and new processes, we will limit what should and could happen when the time for fruit finally arrives. Each day of each season requires unique work to keep up with each new change as our purpose grows through the potential of each season's atmosphere. Remember that God provides the season, but we provide the work.

Summer

As summer comes, the fruit on the tree begins to ripen. Soon, it is ready to pick, and the harvest season has begun. Any farmer will tell you that the season of harvest is the busiest. The crop has a shelf life. It has to be taken in before it goes bad and is wasted.

One of the farmers in my group explained how when he was combining wheat, he kept two combines ready. If one broke down, he would leave it in the field and keep harvesting with the other. He'd fix the broken machine once the harvest was in. He couldn't waste time doing it when the harvest was ripe.

There are seasons like that in our lives, churches, and businesses. There are times when we must work with all our energy to take in the harvest. We make a grave mistake by assuming the harvest, the divine opportunity, will always be there as it is now. When God has given us fruit, we do well to roll up our sleeves and get to work. It must be harvested. That work must be done in that season. There are seasons when the lost are being miraculously saved. There are seasons when profits are pouring in. There are seasons when we reap the benefits of previous hard work.

But the season of harvest can also feel hectic. We don't have time to reorganize or make changes. All our energy is spent keeping up with the work in front of us. I've found that its easy during such times to forget about seasons.

We become overwhelmed, imagining this work will go on forever, or we slow down, imagining we can take our time. Both are mistakes. The season of harvest is one we must take seriously, knowing that this season will end just like all the others.

Fall

Before long, the signs of change come again. The cool mornings and the shifting colors of the leaves are the first signs. The atmosphere is different, and all life must change with it. The fruit is gone, and soon the leaves with it. But don't mistake this season for one of loss. Too many get discouraged and imagine they have moved into a season of failure or loss. They see the harvest ending and imagine they have lost it. But fall has its purposes, just like the seasons before. As the leaves fall from our peach tree, we get our first look at the branches and limbs that have produced all that fruit. And we must take up a new work.

A wise farmer will use this season to prepare for next year's harvest. It's time for the soil to be turned over and prepared. It's time for the branches to be pruned and cut back. In the fall, you can see which new shoots matured and produced fruit, and you can also see which branches are broken or deformed and need to be removed. Pruning, while it feels like cutting and loss, creates the space and order the tree will need for new growth next year. If you prune carefully, you can create the conditions for an even larger harvest in the seasons to come. Your work in the fall is done, trusting that there will be another season of harvest in the future.

The truth is, no person or organization could maintain the pace required by the growth and work that comes in the spring and summer. We all need seasons for pruning and cutting back. In your life, it might mean reworking your schedule and commitments. In an organization, it might be restaffing and reorganizing. The growth of summer fruit can become heavy and out of control. It can outperform the present structure. I have seen the weight of the fruit on a peach tree break the limbs. Just as pruning your peach tree is required, you also need to make cuts once the season shifts from harvest to fall. The fall pruning will ensure you're ready for even more growth next year.

How foolish would it be for a farmer who was watching his fields turn brown and the leaves fall from his orchard panic and conclude his time of productivity was finished? But we do that in our lives and work. It would take even the most inexperienced farmer just one year to recognize that the fading of fall is not failure, but rather the preparations for a still greater harvest.

God has made us to live in seasons. All things are shaped by them. No loss in our lives needs to be final. All things are preparation for the seasons that will come again. Fall is a time to prune, cut, fix what broke during harvest, and prepare by faith for another season of growth and harvest. But even this work comes to an end.

Winter

Winter is the hardest season to recognize God's creative work. The world seems to go dormant—but do not assume this is wasted time. Winter is a chance for our tree to grow deeper, to spread its roots down into the soil, and to anchor itself for new growth.

One winter several years ago, we encountered a home emergency that every homeowner dreads. Our septic system backed up. I called a plumber and stood with him in the yard as he fed his drain-clearing line down into our plumbing. I listened to its drill bit turn and begin to catch. The old plumber began pulling piece after piece of root out of the pipe. "We've never had a problem with roots," I said. "How strange the roots would grow into our pipes during winter."

Kneeling at the hole, the man looked up from his work and said, "You must be a city boy." He went on to explain that winter is exactly the season when roots grow most. We may not see the tree growing above ground, but below ground, winter is all about growth. It's about growing deeper.

We all have seasons in life when nothing seems to be happening. When I was younger, I used to find those seasons frustrating, even discouraging. I didn't understand the opportunity of winter. Winter is a season for each of us to grow deeper. It's a season to read, study, pray, think, clarify, and understand. It's this season that grounds us and allows us to enter the next season with greater wisdom, discernment, and clarity. It's an opportunity to think about what God has done and to discern again the real work before us. I've come to love this season and to value deeply its opportunities. If we neglect the work of this season, our lives will be shallow and easily broken.

I've now lived through enough winters to trust that our tree will bloom again and that God will work new things and new fruit into my life in His time. So, winter is a chance to anchor my life more deeply in Him. Faith makes even winter a season of opportunity.

Discerning the Season You're In

In my experience, each time I teach about the seasons, everyone immediately begins to wonder about which season they are in. You've probably already been doing that as you've been reading. It's an important question. It might be helpful to offer you a single-sentence description of each season to help you discern an answer.

Remember, we are trying to discern the atmosphere God has created around us. Which season you want to be in matters very little. The real question is, what is God doing? So, once again, here are the seasons God both created and uses to work change in your life, family, church, and work.

- Spring: You have new opportunities, new vision, and new energy.
- Summer: You are busy harvesting and taking in new fruit.
- Fall: Growth has slowed, and it's time to prune, cut, and reorganize.
- Winter: Though things feel dormant, there is a pull to go deeper with God, relationships, and all the unseen parts of you.

While in the process of discerning the season you're in, it's also worth remembering that these atmospheres can be different for different parts of your life. Your church may be in one season while you personally are in another. Your work may be in a season that is very different from the season our country is in. That's okay. What's important is that you recognize the season, commit to the work of that season, and trust God to bring the new seasons in His timing. Another observation is that I often find leaders tend to move into the next season just before the church or organization they lead. Recognizing that pattern can help you better prepare the team, family, or congregation for what you have already sensed coming.

This process of discerning and paying attention to the shifting atmosphere of the seasons is a critical skill for everyone, particularly those who are trying to lead and steward the work God is doing. If God is shifting the atmosphere of the season you're in, you, both as an individual and leader, are required to shift, as well.

I can look back on my life and ministry and see very clearly not only the seasons but also the important signs of those seasons changing. I remember one season of harvest in which our church was seeing new believers come to Christ every week. That harvest was uniquely miraculous. There were miracles and divine interventions, and almost every sermon I preached was a message of salvation for the lost. Every week more people responded. The altars were always full. The church was growing, and it felt as if all the dreams and visions I had were finally being fulfilled. I thought it would go on forever. I wanted it to go on forever.

One Sunday night I sat on the steps of the platform as the congregation worshiped and prayed. It had been a long day of ministry and one full of God's miraculous work. Even though the service had been over for some time, the people didn't want to leave. The altars were filled with people who were crying out to God, while others sat in their seats with their faces in their hands. I sat on the steps thinking about all the salvations and miracles we had seen, many that very day. I said to God, very simply, "Thank you." I was so grateful for what was happening.

I heard God answer, *I'm glad you've enjoyed this, but it's time to shift.*

I didn't know what that meant. And I was immediately confused. Shift to what? Wasn't this the goal?

"God, You don't want more of this?" I looked at the people at the altar again and asked, "There isn't more of this?"

That's right, God answered.

I was honest with God and protested, "No. Why would You quit this?"

God carefully explained to me that the church I pastored was about to outgrow its root system. We had experienced so much growth in such a short season that we were at great risk. We didn't realize it, but we were vulnerable. God had given us that growth—it had been a good thing—but by His wisdom, He knew we needed another season to keep it healthy. What God asked me to do was commit to Him and the work that was coming in that next season with the same faithfulness I had given to our season of growth. It was the first time God had spoken to me about seasons.

To be honest, I struggled to understand what God was saying. I hadn't learned about seasons yet. I assumed that success looked like constant accelerating growth. I lacked the wisdom to understand how God used those dependable, repeatable atmospheres to bring real, lasting change. That conversation was a tough way to end a great Sunday. But I recommitted myself to following God regardless of what was to come.

During our season of growth, many leaders and Christian publications came to interview me about how we had created the revival we were experiencing. I didn't have an answer. God had simply changed the atmosphere. I was more than willing to accept that. But suddenly, I faced a new test of accepting the next change of atmosphere God was bringing. There weren't many people interested in how we followed God into that next season of pruning and on into the winter season of growing deeper. But it was through those periods of change that God began to teach me about seasons. Today, that church continues to grow and trusts God's process and timing.

I have found that the changing of seasons is often the hardest to discern. No season changes instantly. It is a process of back and forth. The temperature becomes unstable. The weather patterns fluctuate. We begin to sense that change is near. It's easy to fight the change, not wanting to let go. It is similar in your life and leadership. There are times when, by God's discernment, you will recognize the atmosphere shifting. Though you may love the season you're in, you don't want to miss those signs of change. Recognize them and receive them as new work God is doing.

If you are not deeply grounded in your relationship with God and if you haven't taken the time to understand how God works in seasons, you can become unnerved or frustrated by the changing conditions. They can leave you feeling confused and disoriented. If you grow too attached to any season, the coming change can feel like a failure. But if you learn to recognize how God works in seasons, you will find a sense of peace and joy with each new day. You will learn to trust Him, even as the atmosphere is changing.

Trying to work outside of God's seasons is exhausting. You eventually try to force growth and change that can't grow in the atmosphere you're in. Worse, you take yourself out of the blessing of God's help. Too many leaders try to control the season. Too many believers refuse to follow God into new ones. So, we burn ourselves out. We grow discouraged and disillusioned. We become frustrated and give up. That is not how God intended for us to work. He has created us to work in seasons. And while each season has its work, each season also has its joy and celebrations.

It's no coincidence that the ancient Hebrew people marked the changing of the seasons with religious festivals. They tracked the sun, moon, and stars and anticipated each new season with holidays of worship and sacrifice. They celebrated because God was showing Himself faithful again. We need to rediscover their wisdom. We need to learn to trust and celebrate each of God's seasons. God has chosen to work in seasons not to frustrate us, but so He might sustain growth in us and we might learn to trust Him more.

Whatever season you're in, recognize it and embrace it. Worship God for it. And keep your eyes open for shifts in the atmosphere with which God is moving you into the next seasons of growth and change. God works in the dependable, repeatable atmosphere of each changing season.

Now you can begin to see how God applies His process. He provides seasons of fresh vision and supportive atmospheres to develop new systems and new fruit. He does not do all He intends at once. But rather He gives some of the new shoots and the new fruit a cleansing of last year's producers, deeper roots. Then, He does it all again but at a higher level. Embrace each season because each is important to the final outcome.

> "Let us fear the LORD our God, who gives autumn and spring rains in season, who assures us of the regular weeks of harvest."
>
> Jeremiah 5:24

8

PHASE 5

Addition

And God said, "Let the water teem with living creatures, and let birds fly above the earth across the vault of the sky." So God created the great creatures of the sea and every living thing with which the water teems and that moves about in it, according to their kinds, and every winged bird according to its kind. And God saw that it was good.

—Genesis 1:20–21

By day five of God's creative process, the earth was formed. There was an atmosphere. There were lights marking the passing of seasons. There was water, sky, and ground. There were trees and grasses, plants and flowers, all growing and multiplying. But God was not done. On that fifth day, God added to it. He began to populate the water, sky, and land. He did not draw this new creation only from what existed, but spoke entirely new things into being. This new creation did not form as a process of what came before it, but rather as an unexpected addition to God's previous creation.

Suddenly, those previously created spaces were filled with new things. The oceans teemed with new life. The sky filled with birds, and they began to multiply. What God added began its own process of addition. Genesis 1:22 records that God blessed this new creation and said, "Be fruitful and increase in number and fill the water in the seas, and let the birds increase on the earth." The best word I know for what took place that day is *addition*.

Imagine seeing all that space, that empty canvas of creation, suddenly—or by multiplication, eventually—filled with life of every kind, the birds in all their shapes and colors, and the fish of every size and kind. Had you been there to see it, you would have been in awe of the addition to His already incredible creation. You would have understood something critical about how God's process works. In God's creative process, there is always a day of addition.

Surprisingly, we are not always open to what God wants to add. If we miss this lesson of creation, we are prone to limiting what God wants to add to our lives. We have come a long way in understanding how God is working to change our lives. We have seen new things. We've received new revelations and visions for what our life or church could be. We've implemented new disciplines and embraced the importance of new seasons. But there is a growing temptation to think we've figured this process out. There is a comfort that comes from knowing where we're going and seeing the progress we're making.

Change can feel good when we're watching the trees grow and the plants begin to bloom, when we're observing the rising and setting of the sun. The product of change can be beautiful. But then a day comes when suddenly that perfect scene of new creation is overrun with flocks of birds and swarming fish. Suddenly the tree is having its fruit plucked away. The grass is being trampled, and the peace is broken by endless chirping and squeaking. We aren't sure what to make of it, and everything we've been building suddenly feels at risk. So, we find ourselves wanting to halt what God is adding. We find ourselves wanting to enjoy what we have already built and settle for only a portion of God's process.

There comes a time when God wants to add new things and do unexpected things. Eventually, God asks us to make room for things we have not experienced before. There comes a day of addition when God drops new things into our lives, families, and churches. It will probably feel as though things are getting messed up. New things always leave us worried and afraid. New things always demand change and discomfort. So, we need to recognize that these unexpected additions are an important part of God's process.

God is trying to teach us that we are not enough on our own. We don't have all the resources we need to go where God is taking us. Like it or not, we need these additions. God will inevitably add new people and new things to our lives because it's only by these additions that we can go where God is taking us.

There is a constant temptation to think we have everything we need. There is a temptation to think that we are enough. That all we need is more of the same. If we lack something, we want God to produce it from what we already have. We want Him to give us new talents, new possessions, and new gifts. At times, God does that, but more often, He brings along a new person who has what we need. That requires us not only to recognize we need it, but also to be willing to receive it from someone or something new.

Make no mistake: God has carefully designed and intentionally formed us. The Bible uses the language of God knitting us together in our mother's womb. Our talents, gifts, personalities, and skills are not random. God has made us. Everything God makes is created with purpose and intentionality. We like thinking about the gifts and talents God has given us. But if God is intentional about those talents He gives, then He is also intentional about the talents He withholds. We have some things, but there are other things that weren't given to us.

We were not designed to be self-sufficient. We were not designed to reach the end by ourselves. In fact, God has called us to do things we do not have the resources to complete by ourselves. God has designed us to need each other. As God said early in Genesis 2:18, "It is not good for the man to be alone." God has designed us with something to offer, and He has designed us with limits that will require us to receive new things from new people.

The Surprise of God's Addition

Peter was a devout Jew. He understood and lived faithfully by the Jewish laws. Even after leaving his fishing boats to follow Jesus, Peter continued living by the Mosaic law. It's clear in the Gospels that God was leading Peter through a process of new creation. Peter got so much right but also got a lot wrong. Yet Jesus continued to teach him. Peter was changing. He was in Jesus' discipleship process and becoming a new creation. On the day of Pentecost, Peter, who once was afraid to admit he was a follower of Jesus, suddenly found the boldness to preach about Jesus before the gathered crowd. He called them to repentance, and thousands were saved.

The Spirit had come upon Peter, and Peter was forever changed by it. God had long been working that process in Peter's life. Peter might have thought of his new courage and boldness brought about by this new gift, this addition of the Holy Spirit, as the end of that process. It was a decisive moment of change for him. After all, he had not only been one of the apostles selected by Christ but had also emerged as one of the key leaders of the early Church. But there was more God wanted to do. There were things God still wanted to add.

The book of Acts records that one day, while traveling, Peter went up on the roof of a house to rest and pray (see Acts 10). While praying, Peter became hungry. He could probably smell the meal being prepared in the house below. As a Jew, Peter observed a careful diet that conformed to Jewish law. What he ate was one of the many ways that he differentiated himself from the pagan gentile world. As

Peter prayed and felt his hunger grow, Acts records that he fell into a trance. Peter began to have a vision.

Above him, he saw the heavens opening and a large sheet being let down from above. As he watched the sheeting descend, he saw that it was full of all the unclean animals that the Jewish law prohibited him from eating. There were all kinds of unclean four-footed animals, reptiles, and birds. Peter must have recognized right away that these were the foods eaten by gentiles. He knew, without any hesitation, that those were the foods he would never consume.

Yet Peter heard a voice from heaven say, "Get up, Peter. Kill and eat" (Acts 10:13). Peter was shocked and immediately objected.

"'Surely not, Lord!' Peter replied. 'I have never eaten anything impure or unclean'" (v. 14).

But the voice from heaven answered, "Do not call anything impure that God has made clean" (v. 15).

Three times that conversation repeated itself. Peter couldn't make sense of it. He couldn't accept it. Then Peter watched the sheet ascend again into heaven, and his vision was over. While Peter wondered about what had happened, three men came to the house looking for him. They were gentiles, and they wanted Peter to go with them. The Spirit moved on Peter's heart, and he began to understand. God was calling him to take the gospel to those gentiles.

Peter had seen God's power and the impact of Jesus' ministry. He had seen how the Spirit was at work changing his own life and the lives of thousands around him. Peter understood much about what God was doing and how He was doing it. But even Peter was surprised by what God was adding. Unlike the constant teaching from Jesus about the coming gift of the Spirit, the inclusion of gentiles was completely unexpected and very uncomfortable. Jesus had not prepared them for this with the same clarity He had the Spirit. What God is adding to our lives may sometimes seem just as uncomfortable, but before we scream *unclean*, we should pray and ask. It may be God.

The early Church struggled to incorporate the number of gentiles who were coming to faith. It was hard because their presence did change things and didn't fit the patterns or forms to which they had become accustomed. God was adding new people to His Church, and it would mean new complexities and challenges for leaders like Peter. But Peter, sensitive to the Spirit and committed to prayer, was able to recognize it. That realization wasn't easy, but Peter began to sense that the Church was entering a new phase in which God was working new and unexpected additions.

The early Church could have shut the door. They could have refused the gentiles. They could have held onto all the great things they had experienced. They could have protected those things by refusing anything new. Thank goodness, though, that they were willing to trust all of God's process. Thank goodness they understood the challenge but also the purpose of God's additions. They set an early example for discerning and trusting God's process.

The first and most challenging lesson we need to learn is to expect God to bring along new things. We cannot allow ourselves to get comfortable with what we have presently. We should recognize our limits and recognize our needs. And recognize that God will usually solve it by bringing someone new. Expect there to be new perspectives. Expect there to be new opinions. Expect people to have new ways of doing things. That's exactly what we need. This process of growth through addition is critical to continue growing in God's process.

Later in the New Testament, it was Peter who made this point. Peter encouraged believers to:

> Make every effort to add to your faith goodness; and to goodness, knowledge; and to knowledge, self-control; and to self-control, perseverance; and to perseverance, godliness; and to godliness, mutual affection; and to mutual affection, love. For if you possess these qualities in increasing measure, they will keep you from being ineffective and unproductive in your knowledge of our Lord Jesus Christ. But whoever does not have them is nearsighted and blind, forgetting that they have been cleansed from their past sins.
>
> 2 Peter 1:5–9

Do you see the process of addition in Peter's teaching? Peter encourages us to add new things to our faith. Peter used a strong and active word. This adding he describes is not passive or apathetic. We are to seek this addition eagerly. There is something we are supposed to do. What we have is not enough. We must add to it. There is an aggressiveness to this work.

Faith is belief, but Peter expects us to add goodness to that faith. Goodness is action. It isn't enough to just believe. We add work, practice, and action. To that action, we must also seek to add knowledge. Knowledge comes through prayer, discernment, learning, and listening. Knowledge requires humility. And as we learn, we also recognize things we need. Then, we must add new levels of self-control. These additions begin to build up to new things that require perseverance, Peter's next point. There is a process forming.

And look at where these additions inevitably lead us. We must move from personal faith and self-control toward mutual affection and love. How does God work that process? He brings new people into our lives. Love requires others. Mutual affection requires new people. God has designed this process to open our lives to others. Eventually, the process ends up with us loving others and receiving from them new things in return.

Look at the results Peter describes. It is through this broadening process of new people and new pursuits that we become more productive and increase in effectiveness. We don't do it on our own. We do it best with others.

If you want to do more for God, it will require new people. If you want to be effective in all God has called you to, it will require the help of others. And Peter also offers a warning. If you refuse this lesson, if you refuse to open your life to new people, you only reveal that you are nearsighted and blind. You forget where this process started. You forget how you have been cleansed of sin and called by God. That's to say that if God can use you, He can use others. If God has called you, He has also called others. This whole process started with you needing things you couldn't produce on your own. You need God, and the process continues as God meets those needs through the lives of others.

The truth is, we need each other. You might not like it, but that is how God is working in us. This process of creation is not just about you. Because you can't get where God is taking you without opening your life to the gifts and support of other believers. You need God to add to your life. He does it through others.

It's Hard to Hear the Truth

I have never had a vision of sheets of meat descending from heaven, but I've certainly experienced God stretching my expectations and challenging my assumptions. I know how hard it can be to hear this word of addition. As a young pastor, I thought I knew a lot about growing a church. I had a vision, and I had a plan. I remember one morning going into prayer feeling highly motivated and filled with faith. I was praying that our church would experience new growth and breakthroughs.

We were just under one hundred members, and I believed God would give us growth to break through that plateau. I had faith for it. I had vision for it. I was working hard to see it happen. And I prayed with real boldness. I was actually impressed with my prayer that morning. I thought I must be praying in line with God's will. I assumed God was impressed with my prayer, as well. Then I heard God say something to me as strange as Peter's vision must have been to him.

How can I pour ten gallons of water into an eight-ounce cup? Like Peter, I was confused. What did that mean? I asked God to explain it to me, and He certainly did. It was not easy to hear. He was trying to add something I hadn't even realized I needed.

God said, *Rick, you are an eight-ounce preacher wanting a ten-gallon blessing.* And He repeated His question. *How can I pour ten gallons of water into an eight-ounce cup?*

I understood His point. I was no longer very impressed with my prayer. And I knew right away that He was right. The truth is, I was so focused on what I thought God wanted to do and how I was going to get there that I had lost sight of the things missing in my life. I had lost sight of my own limitations and my need for help. I thought I had everything we needed. I didn't realize what was missing. I didn't realize what God wanted to add.

It easily happens to all of us. Fired up and filled with faith, we take off after the things we want God to do. In our assumptions, we can miss the days of addition along the way in which God uses unexpected means and unexpected people to get us there. That day in prayer, God forced my attention to change. He forced me to open my life to what He wanted to add. God explained that He had new people He was going to bring into my life. These people would come with new ways of thinking, new processes, and new ideas. I needed to be humble enough to learn from them.

There is an important reason this lesson often comes on day five of God's process. In the beginning, we're usually open to new things, but as we begin to make progress, we start to trust ourselves more than God. We become increasingly confident in what we think we know. As we have success, we begin to overestimate our own knowledge and abilities. The further we get down God's creative process, the greater the temptation we have to think we've figured it out. So, it is usually here, about day five, that God drops new things to disrupt our comfort. It's here, about day five, that He adds things that make us uncomfortable and force us to trust Him again.

Do you remember Jesus' parable of the bags of gold (see Matthew 25)? Jesus told the story of a wealthy man going away on a trip. Before he left, he gathered his servants. To one of them, he gave five bags of gold. To another, he gave two bags. And to the final servant, he gave just one bag of gold. Upon leaving, the first two men went to work, investing the gold they had received. Upon the master's return, the servants came to report on what had been given to them and what they had done with it. The man with five bags had invested it and had earned five more. Likewise, the man with two bags had earned two more.

Finally, the steward who had been given just one bag of gold approached the master. He explained that he had not invested it but had buried his gold for safekeeping. So, he presented the master with only the single original bag he had received. How did he explain his decision? "'Master,' he said, 'I knew that you are a hard man, harvesting where you have not sown and gathering where you have not scattered seed. So, I was afraid and went out and hid your gold in the ground'" (Matthew 25:24–25).

First, we should note the man's fear. He was afraid of his master and unwilling to risk anything. He hoarded what he had because of this fear. But he also said something equally interesting. The man described his master as one who harvested where he had not sown and gathered where he had not scattered seed. This made the servant nervous. He didn't understand how his master worked, and so he trusted no one but himself. He held on to what he had. He hid his treasure away. He lived in apprehension. But the very quality of his master that made him nervous allowed the other servants to see an opportunity.

The other servants, like their master, invested and earned a reward greater than their original possession. They risked giving their gold to others who could add to it. Because of their risk, they received a profit in return. Through the parable, Jesus described how His Kingdom worked and how His servants should work. Our lives and our faith are dependent on others. We have heard the gospel because someone else sowed and others harvested. As Paul later explained, some had planted, some had watered, and some had harvested (see 1 Corinthians 3:6). Our salvation is owed to countless men and women who have risked and invested their lives before us.

God does not ask us to be all things, to know all things, or to do all things. But He does ask us to give what we have and be willing to receive from others. We also reap where we have not sown and gather where we have not planted. We are designed to receive from others, to be blessed by others, and to be multiplied by the gifts of others. So, we should be willing to take those risks ourselves. We should give, and we should receive. That's how things grow in God's Kingdom.

But to do that, we cannot live in fear. We cannot, like the third servant, hide ourselves away and play it safe. In Jesus' parable, the master had hard words for that servant. The master replied, "You wicked, lazy servant! So you knew that I harvest where I have not sown and gather where I have not scattered seed? Well then, you should have put my money on deposit with the bankers, so that when I returned I would have received it back with interest" (Matthew 25:26–30). The man's mistake was trying to protect himself and what he had. He risked nothing, and so he gained nothing. The process of creation and growth was cut short.

Likewise, you possess a bag of gold. Maybe not literally, but God has entrusted you with valuable things. They have been given to you by your Master. Sure, some people have more bags, some fewer, but in the end, that is not what matters. The wealth you have been given is your talents, gifts, time, and resources. God has entrusted them to you. You can decide what you will do with that wealth.

Many will choose, as the wicked servant did, to live in fear. They will horde what they have. They will bury their time and talents for themselves. They will refuse to risk losing any of it, believing that if they can just keep what they have, it will be enough. But God did not give us this treasure to protect it. He gave it to us so that we might use it, even risk it. That is how God works. God invests His treasure into the lives of others and receives from it a greater return.

Those who recognize this attribute in God will live like Him. Those who understand the parable will take whatever talents and gifts they possess and give them away. By their giving, they will open their lives to receive from others. Give away ten bags of gold, and we'll get it all back with ten more in surplus. That's the lesson of the parable.

There is risk. There is always risk in investing. But that is the only way to grow. Hoarding and hiding never produce anything new. So, you have a choice to make. What will you do with what you have been given? What are you willing to risk?

There is another way to ask that question. Are you seeing a return on your current investment? Is God depositing new things in your life? When was the last time God added something unexpected to your life? Were you willing to receive it? Did you recognize that you needed it?

If you are not experiencing new things or people—sometimes unexpected or uncomfortable additions—perhaps you are living too safely. Maybe you are not opening your life to all that God wants to do. You might be missing out on the gift of God's addition. There is a risk, but there is an even greater reward.

Two things are required. You must be willing to give what you have, and you must be willing to receive what others have. That means showing up. It means serving and receiving. How many times has someone needed what you had but you didn't speak up? And perhaps someone was prepared to offer you exactly what you needed, but you stayed home. The full blessing of what God wants to do depends on you opening your life to others. That is the law of addition. God wants to do new things, but it will require new people, new perspectives, and new ideas. It will require you to make room in your heart and mind for what God wants to add.

Don't get stuck. Don't grow blind. Don't assume you know what God is doing. Add to your faith. Open your life to God's additions. Embrace the risk and the discomfort and see what new things God is preparing to do.

"See, I am doing a new thing! Now it springs up; do you not perceive it? I am making a way in the wilderness and streams in the wasteland."

Isaiah 43:19

PHASE 6 (PART 1)

Opposition

And God said, "Let the land produce living creatures according to their kinds: the livestock, the creatures that move along the ground, and the wild animals, each according to its kind.". . . And God saw that it was good.

—Genesis 1:24–25

On day five, God created new kinds of living creatures—the livestock and the roaming wild animals. As He had populated the sky and sea days before, so He populated the land with every kind of living thing. God's creation took on a new kind of order. There were animals to eat the grass and fruit, and there were animals to eat those animals. A careful balance of life emerged that helped control the populations of these new herds and controlled the growing plants of the land. But God's creation also took on a new complexity.

With God's new creation of animals came a new reality: opposition. These animals knew how to run, fight, and attack. They introduced a new kind of opposition to creation. It was a lesson in which humanity would soon become a participant. It might seem surprising to see opposition in those early days of God's creation, and it might seem even more surprising to suggest that God called that opposition good, but that is only because we fail to recognize God's purposes in the opposition we face. Opposition is a part of the process of creation God uses to bring about what is good. It may be uncomfortable, it may even be difficult, but opposition is a part of God's process. It was true on that sixth day of creation, and it is true today in your life. God works all things for the good of those He has called. But He often works that good through the experience of opposition.

Have you ever considered that God created the serpent? The serpent was in the garden even before Adam and Eve's fall. The serpent was there with his lying words and temptation even before their disobedience. Even in the goodness of the garden, humanity faced an adversary. There was opposition to God's word and command even in paradise. But that opposition was never a threat to God's creation. It was a part of His process. Even in the garden, God had a plan for how He would use that opposition.

In the New Testament, Peter reminded the Church:

> Be alert and of sober mind. Your enemy the devil prowls around like a roaring lion looking for someone to devour. Resist him, standing firm in the faith, because you know

that the family of believers throughout the world is undergoing the same kind of sufferings.

1 Peter 5:8–9

It's no coincidence that the devil is compared to one of those roaming beasts created on the sixth day. He is our opponent. As in the garden, we still face an adversary. For all that God has done and is doing, we still have the devil as an enemy. And like those wild beasts God created, the devil prowls like a roaring lion.

God does not warn us about the devil simply to remind us that the devil exists. God warns us because we continue to face opposition from him. God tells us about our opponent so that we might recognize and embrace the way that opposition matures us and works in God's process. I want to show you two important things opposition does so that you might come to see the goodness of opposition in your life. Our opponent is not good, but even in his scheming and his threats, God can still work good for us. Isn't that good news? Ours is a God who uses even the work of our opponent for our good. Let me show you how.

God Calls Opposition Good

The first thing opposition can do is turn your attention to God. Though Adam and Eve were seduced by the serpent's words, Eve's conversation with the serpent had been an opportunity to turn their attention back to God and all God had given them. It's no coincidence that the serpent first sought to undermine God's credibility. The serpent knew that his temptations risked turning humanity toward God. But he was shrewd, and he instead led Eve to turn away from God and toward herself. When we face opposition, we face the same choice. We can turn away from God or recognize each opposition as an opportunity to discover God's power in new ways.

It's an old saying that there are no atheists in foxholes. Sometimes it takes opposition to get our attention. Many people would never give God attention if it were not for the challenges they faced in life. Without opposition, we tend to become self-absorbed. Without opposition, we think we are self-sufficient. When everything is easy and goes our way, we tend to forget about God.

Do you remember when Israel was just about to enter the promised land? Moses gave them a long sermon recorded in the book of Deuteronomy. They had spent a generation being led through the wilderness by a pillar of fire. They had faced all kinds of opposition, from hunger to the raiding parties of rival neighbors. If not for miraculous provision and protection, they never would have made it out of the desert alive. Though they often complained and grumbled, God was constantly making His presence known through their needs. But Moses knew a new temptation awaited them in the promised land.

> When the LORD your God brings you into the land he swore to your fathers, to Abraham, Isaac and Jacob, to give you—a land with large, flourishing cities you did not build, houses filled with all kinds of good things you did not provide, wells you did not dig, and vineyards and

olive groves you did not plant—then when you eat and are satisfied, be careful that you do not forget the LORD.

Deuteronomy 6:10–12

They had dreamed their whole lives of a homeland. They had dreamed of life in that land flowing with milk and honey. They had probably prayed countless prayers for a house, a vineyard, a fresh well, and peace. All of it was about to be theirs by God's miraculous provision. If all your prayers were answered miraculously, wouldn't you spend every day thanking God for it? Moses recognized that is not how our broken human attention works. Once we get what we want, we tend to forget about God. It's sad to read that the people did not remember Moses' warning. Once they began to prosper in their new land, they forgot God and started worshiping all the idols of their neighbors.

I wonder if you recognize this tendency in your life. You are certainly praying for things. You're reading this book because you're trusting God to give you new visions and to bring about those miraculous changes in your life, family, and church. But can I warn you, as Moses did Israel, there is danger in getting everything you want just as you want it. It is possible that you might receive great miracles from God and then forget about Him entirely.

One of the reasons God continues to allow opposition is so that we continue to turn to Him. He lets us face challenges so that our faith might stay sharp and alive. He lets us remember through difficulties how much we need Him. Opposition is one of God's tools to keep us from falling away. But there is also a second reason God allows us to face opposition. God also allows opposition so that we might learn to fight.

It is easy for us to grow spiritually lazy. It's easy for our faith to atrophy. Where we once believed for great things, we can eventually settle for far less. Where once we fought a good fight by faith, we can surrender and accept things as just the way they are. We can lose our ability to fight. Our weapons grow dull. Our bodies lose their strength, and our courage to press on fades. God, in His goodness, brings about an opponent to reenergize our faith.

There is a very strange prophecy in Isaiah that makes this point. The prophet stated:

> "See, it is I who created the blacksmith
> who fans the coals into flame
> and forges a weapon fit for its work.
> And it is I who have created the destroyer to wreak
>   havoc;
> no weapon forged against you will prevail,
> and you will refute every tongue that accuses you."
> Isaiah 54:16–17

Isaiah notes that it is God who has created the destroyer who wreaks havoc. Is that surprising to you? Remember, it was God who created the serpent. But read carefully. Though God has created the opponent, the opponent's weapons cannot prevail against you. God has created you for the fight, but He has not created you to lose that fight. God has created you to be victorious by faith. Isaiah makes this point clear in another verse from the same chapter. Speaking through the prophet, God reminded His people,

"If anyone does attack you, it will not be my doing; whoever attacks you will surrender to you" (Isaiah 54:15).

God is not our opponent. Don't mistake His use of opposition for Him being that opposition. When we face opposition and struggle, it is not God who opposes us. We should be very clear about that. It is God who gives us victory and brings our enemies to their knees in surrender. God is the source of our strength, but to build that strength, He does use opposition. He changes us through opposition. The weapons of the enemy are not designed to destroy you. They are allowed by God to awaken you and strengthen your faith. God uses opposition for your good.

Once you recognize this principle, you are equipped with a powerful tool for facing opposition in your life, family, or church. Many people run from challenges. As leaders, we sometimes think that opposition is a sign of our failure. We think that we should be able to plan and organize our way out of any challenge. But that is not how God grows us. Once we learn to see opposition as a part of God's process, we will be freed from the lies of fear and discouragement, and it will embolden us to fight the good fight by faith. Instead of running, we'll be prepared to lead our churches, our families, our businesses, and ourselves.

Opposition turns our attention to God and sharpens our weapons of faith. Opposition intensifies our prayers and clarifies our sight. Opposition produces heroes of faith.

Those Who Face Opposition

Consider for a moment all the great men and women of faith we read about in the Bible. Think of those individuals whose character you would most like to imitate. Think of those men and women who lived by faith and sacrifice. They lived lives with courage and boldness. As I read their stories, one of the most common elements throughout the biblical narrative is the presence of real opposition in their lives. Open your Bible to almost any story and you will find a man or woman of God who faced opposition. I want to suggest that their greatness of faith was not in spite of that opposition but because of it.

What would Joseph's story have meant if he had never been attacked or sold into slavery by his brothers? What would his character have been if he had never been falsely accused by his master's wife or spent years struggling in an Egyptian prison? We know Joseph's story because he faced great opposition, and during that opposition, he lived by faith and overcame it. It was opposition that made his life heroic.

Or consider the story of Esther. What do we remember of Esther? It is not just her beauty or the Persian palace in which she lived. Those weren't the qualities that defined her. Esther is remembered for her courage in the face of opposition. Against all the power of Persia and facing the penalty of death, she risked everything to save her people. What would her story have been if not for that opposition?

Opposition is present in every story of the Bible and in every great person of faith. Shadrach, Meshach, and Abednego are remembered for their faith even facing a furnace. Daniel prayed as he was thrown in the den of lions. David was hunted in caves even after having been anointed king. Paul faced beatings and shipwreck. Peter was said to have been crucified upside down.

We all want to be Joseph, Daniel, Esther, or Paul. Yet none of us wants to be betrayed, thrown in prison, threatened with death, shipwrecked on deserted islands, or cast into a den of lions. But perhaps it takes great opposition to produce great faith. Perhaps that kind of faith can only be created in times of great challenge.

Without opposition, the biblical stories would be flat and unfulfilling. Without opposition, there would be no need for faith, and there would be nothing to encourage us in our faith. Most of us want to live like the great heroes of Scripture, but we don't want to face opposition.

I know that even as you are reading this you may be facing very real opposition in your life. I don't want to dismiss it or lead you to believe that it cannot be overcome. God has promised you victory. But what I want you to recognize is that opposition is not evidence of God's absence. Opposition is not evidence of a failure in God's plans. Opposition does not mean the change God has been working in you is suddenly lost. Opposition is how God is bringing about that change. Opposition is how God is growing you in faith and offering you more of His power and presence. Opposition is a key stage of God's creative process.

While God may allow you to face more opposition than you would like, know this: He will not let you be defeated by it. Greater is He who is in you than he who is in the world (see 1 John 4:4). While you may face a great opponent, you possess an even greater God. Your opponent is destined to fail, and you will be made greater for having endured the test.

The Problem We Face

We live in a time when very few Christians still see the value of opposition. We simply do not want to fight. We will do almost anything to avoid opposition. Because of this, I fear we are greatly reducing what God wants to do in us and through us.

I grew up at a time in American culture when being a Christian was widely accepted and respected. It was also easy, and I think many believers and churches got comfortable. We lived off the victories won by previous generations. We benefited from their fights of faith. And in the comfort we inherited, we forgot how to fight. We became more consumed with our personal property than with the power of God in our lives. The evidence of our drift is everywhere in the Church. Prayer meetings have decreased in popularity. The genuine study of the Word has been replaced by feel-good preaching. Worship has become more about style than creating time to encounter the Holy Spirit. The Church's loss of faith allowed our culture to drift away from God. But there is a shift taking place.

Today, the Church is facing new opposition. While some are gripped with fear because of it, I believe God is using this new opposition to turn us again to His power and reawaken a new fight of faith. We now find ourselves in a time when being a Christian carries no credibility and is often seen as a negative. The culture, our school systems, and many government leaders are now open opponents to the Church and biblical teaching. So, this opposition is driving the Church back to the altar. It is teaching us to pray again. It is forcing us to find new boldness and stamina. God is not our opponent, but He is using this new opposition to strengthen His Church. God is using these new times of opposition to renew our faith.

As we grow in the true grace and power of God, as we remember that our weapons are not like those of this world, and as we take on the strongholds of our ultimate opponent, the devil himself, we will find ourselves changed. We will discover that this fight has drawn us closer to God, and, like so many of the witnesses of Scripture, our lives will take on a greater spiritual significance.

The real problem our nation is facing is not our opponents. The real problem we face is that we have forgotten what we have by the Spirit, and we have forgotten how to fight. When we go too long without a battle, we become weak in our worship, walk, faith, and practice of true Christianity. But that is not true only of the American Church, it is also true in your life. You are constantly at risk of settling for less than God has for you. You are often at risk of giving up on God's process before He has completed His work in you.

I wonder if the opposition you are facing right now has caused you to turn away from God. I wonder if you are settling for less. I wonder if you have given up just when God is calling you to fight. The opposition you're facing may simply be the next step in God's process of change in your life.

The Fights We Face

There are two kinds of battles we need to be prepared to fight. First, long before any major battle, there are skirmishes. Skirmishes do not destroy nations, but they can have a profound effect on morale and preparation.

Skirmishes often come as a surprise. The enemy will make an unexpected attack and withdraw just as quickly. While nothing major is lost, these encounters leave us discouraged and burnt out. They wear us down.

We have all faced them. Small moments of opposition that distort our mood, distract our prayers, and leave us discouraged. At times, we fail to recognize the real source of these attacks. They weaken our faith while never showing themselves to be true opposition. We must learn to pay attention to this strategy of the enemy. Though small, these microfrustrations can be dangerous; however, they can also be continual opportunities for us to grow and strengthen our faith.

Learn to think of these small skirmishes as practice and preparation for greater opposition to come. Learn how to fight these battles by prayer, faith, and confidence in God. Do not grow weary. Turn your attention to the things above. Dwell on what is good. Learn to live in gratitude even when skirmishes come. Taking the time to recognize these skirmishes and learn from them can be an important tool God uses to develop your faith. I think that, like our daily exercise and diet, these small spiritual battles are an important part of growing and maturing as a believer. They are how God changes you.

But there are often much greater battles to be faced. Occasionally the enemy attacks, not just to annoy us, but to try to knock us off the hill. There are attacks meant to bring us down. Satan not only wants to distract us, but he also wants to destroy our faith. We must be prepared to fight these battles. I have found that the greatest need in these conflicts is perseverance. The devil's goal is to make us surrender our faith or give up on things we've spent years praying for. The battle is never the time to surrender.

Sometimes these full-scale attacks can last for months, years, or even a lifetime. While the dangers are real, these tests have the potential to produce remarkable faith and boldness in the life of a believer. As a pastor, I have often watched God's people face incredibly difficult challenges, and while some have given up their faith, I have seen many others manifest remarkable courage and boldness that no opponent could destroy. It seemed to me that the greater the opposition, the greater the faith that emerged.

I want faith like that. I want a faith that cannot be shaken. I want a faith that pushes back the darkness. I want a faith that endures as a testament to my children and grandchildren. I want a faith that wages war in the heavens and sees earthly kingdoms brought low. But I am not naïve enough to think that that kind of faith can be developed in a recliner or in some hammock on the beach. Great faith is cultivated in the midst of great opposition. We grow in faith as we fight. Remind yourself again of James's words.

> Consider it pure joy, my brothers and sisters, whenever you face trials of many kinds, because you know that the testing of your faith produces perseverance. Let perseverance finish its work so that you may be mature and complete, not lacking anything.
>
> James 1:2–4

Remind yourself who has let you face this opposition. He does not seek your destruction, but your good. God is for you, even during great challenges. What you are experiencing is not designed for your defeat, but for your faith. It was designed for the glory of the God, who will see that you not only make it through, but that you stand victorious with Him in the end.

There is no opposition or opponent we face that will not be subdued in the end. There is no victory that will not be ours. And there will be no price paid that will not ultimately be worth every penny.

The night Jesus was betrayed, He warned His disciples about what lay ahead. In a few hours, He would be arrested. He would be handed over to the authorities to be executed. His own disciples, like sheep, would scatter and abandon Him. But in three days, Jesus would be raised from the dead. The Gospels record that Jesus told them these things so that they might have peace. Jesus told them about the opposition to come so that they might find peace amid those challenges.

I hope this chapter, this stage of God's creative work in your life, will do the same. I hope learning to see the opposition you face and the one who has overcome it will give you that same peace and perseverance. There are so many good things God has in store for you. Do not let your heart grow fearful. Do not be anxious. Even in the face of trouble, believe, seek God, and pray. For even this moment of opposition, by God's creative work, can be for your good.

"In this world you will have trouble. But take heart! I have overcome the world."

John 16:33

PHASE 6 (PART 2)

Authority

Then God said, "Let us make mankind in our image, in our likeness, so that they may rule over the fish in the sea and the birds in the sky, over the livestock and all the wild animals, and over all the creatures that move along the ground."

—Genesis 1:26

Day six was the only day that God took on two creative tasks. As we saw in the last chapter, day six began with the creation of animals—the beasts and the livestock of the land. But God did not end there. On day six, He also created humanity. And in a way equally unique to that final day of creation, God established a purpose for His new creation. God gave humanity a task and the authority to accomplish it.

What God was building gained momentum as the days passed. The pace increased as the animals filled the land and continued with the formation of a man from the ground and a woman from his side. It's easy to see the pattern of creation that took place on each previous day, but the sixth day broke that pattern. Not only did God create twice on that day, but He also revealed the reason for His creation in a way He hadn't before. Why did God create this universe? Why did He form atmosphere, seasons, and life?

Genesis 1:26 records the unique reason for God's creation: "Let us make mankind in our image, in our likeness, so that they may rule over the fish in the sea and the birds in the sky, over the livestock and all the wild animals, and over all the creatures that move along the ground." God culminated His creation with a declaration of purpose. Everything had been created so that humanity might take up the work of ruling over it. God had created not only for Himself, but so that He might share creation—both its joys and responsibilities—with us.

Genesis also records God's direct command to the first couple to take up that work: "God blessed them and said to them, 'Be fruitful and increase in number; fill the earth and subdue it. Rule over the fish in the sea and the birds in the sky and over every living creature that moves on the ground'" (1:28). With that command, there was a passing to humanity of what had been God's. We were not just created—we were created to participate and rule with God.

The same God who had spoken light into darkness and formed the vast spaces of sky, ocean, and land finally entrusted that creation to the humanity He had placed at its center. It is a powerful image and a sober reality. We share the responsibility of caring for God's creation.

It is not hard to recognize what God does for us. It can be harder to recognize what God is asking us to do. We want to receive from God, but too many are reluctant to step into the authority and responsibility of God's calling for us to give back to creation. The final act of God's creative process is a statement of our calling to serve. The world is ours to bless or to curse.

One of the most common objections to faith is the condition of our world. People look around and wonder how a loving God could allow so much suffering, sickness, and conflict. We imagine that a good God would just fix it or never have created such a mess at all. But that question misses a far more important point. God has set out to fix the world. He has determined to do it through us. And He has promised us all the power and authority we need.

The condition of the world has more to say about our reluctance to fulfill our responsibility than God's. We are reluctant to take on these responsibilities, to rule and subdue the earth as God intended. We receive from God but fail to recognize that with great gifts come great responsibilities. The condition of our world is evidence of *our* failures and faults, not God's. Seeing the brokenness of the world should turn us with humility to God. Perhaps God is waiting to give us just what this world needs. He is asking you to help Him bring salvation and restoration.

God does not create for Himself alone. He built His creation so that He could give it away to us. God shares what He has created. And He calls us to participate with Him in stewarding and ruling over it. That task can sound overwhelming. We don't imagine we can fix what is broken. But God has prepared us for that work. He has changed us and given us all the authority we need to lead well. In fact, God works in our lives precisely because He wants to use us in the process of reaching the world.

What does it mean to subdue and rule over creation? It means we bear responsibility for the world around us. God not only does things for us, but He also gives us areas of responsibility in which we are to rule and give increase. Pay attention to the places God has given you authority. As a follower of Jesus, you carry His power and authority into dark places. You speak His good news into your workplace, family, church, neighborhood, and community. I find most people underestimate the potential impact of their lives. They neglect the authority God is giving them for where He has placed them.

Through the past chapters, we've seen how God works on our behalf. We've seen how He gives us vision, how He changes the atmosphere of our situations, and how He guides us in this process of change. But you would be mistaken to think that you are passive in this process, or that it has been primarily about you at all. It takes faith to follow God through His process of change. To arrive at the end is to realize that change now requires new responsibilities. What God has been doing in you has been preparing you to bless others. He has been increasing your ability to walk correctly in your authority.

Don't let that overwhelm you. You do not take up that work alone. Look again at the task God gave Adam and Eve. They were to subdue creation, ruling over the birds, fish, and animals. We know from later passages that this also included the toil of tilling the ground, planting, and harvesting. Much of that work is accounted for in God's days of creation. He filled the sky, water, and ground and then asked us to care for it. But those tasks do not include all of God's work. God has reserved work for His own responsibility. God continues to move the sun and stars through the sky. He maintains the regular turning of the seasons and the atmosphere above. So, our work becomes dependent on His work. We are to share in this work. We need what only He can do, and He has entrusted His resources and abilities to us.

There is always a calling at the end of God's creative process. Change always leads to new authority and responsibility. I wonder if you can recognize that new calling and authority forming in the change God has been working in your life. Whatever God is doing in you is to prepare you to serve others.

The Fruit Is Also Seed

Now is a good time for us to reflect on and take inventory of what God has been doing in our lives, family, and church. We began this book by looking at the darkness and chaos that existed before creation. We recognize that the same chaos often exists in our own lives. But it's into this mess that God speaks, and the light of new revelation begins to push back the darkness. We saw how God

begins to shape the atmosphere, creating the conditions
for that revelation to grow and clarify. We then discussed
how new revelation requires new structures in life. The
change God is creating requires change in our own lives.
Structure gives way to seasons in which we begin to experience the growth and harvest of what God designed. We
saw how new things form and how God adds to our lives.
Even through opposition, we are refined and strengthened.

So, now is the time to look back and recognize what
God has done. How has God been changing you? How has
He challenged you? And perhaps most important, what
now exists that didn't before? By God's creative process,
something is now yours that wasn't before. Learning to
recognize what God has done is key to learning to steward
and use it. With every change come new tasks and a new
calling.

Adam and Eve were not given creation simply to enjoy
its fruit or to walk around looking at it. They were given
creation so that they might serve God through their work
in it. They received it and took responsibility. That is also
true for you and what God has been producing in your life.
Whatever God is doing in your life, you can be sure He is
doing it not only for your benefit, but so that you might use
it to serve others and steward the place He has given you.

As we near the end of God's creative work and the end
of this book, it's easy to think that the process is over. But
that is the wrong way of looking at it. The end of God's
creative process is really another beginning. God is now
asking you to use what He has given you and taught you
to help others. Change in us is a preparation for service
from us. What God gives becomes the means by which you

give back. The first time God used His creative process, there was no person or other life form. He did it uninterrupted and without the participation of others. The first time Adam participated with God was when God told him to name the animals. Every time since then, God has worked with and through people. Once He gave creation to humanity, He never usurped or bypassed that authority. Now that He has provided the light, and by it divine revelation, we can choose to respond or not. Now that He has provided the atmosphere, we must decide to take advantage of it. We must be willing to follow His nudge to restructure. We must use the season and make room for the new gifts He provides.

But that's not all. When He is about to start a new process of transformation of a church, family, city, or nation, He calls someone to lead it. Just as He sent John the Baptist to bring new revelation before the coming of Jesus, just as He sent Nehemiah to provide revelation to Israel so they could build the wall, and just as He sent Paul to bring revelation to the gentiles, He uses us to open the eyes of those blinded by dysfunction, lies, and sin to help them understand atmospheres and seasons.

As He used others to help you see what had been hidden from you, He now wants to use you for others. God controls the seasons and the atmospheres, but we control the seeds. He gives seed to the sower, who is us!

But there is another warning we need to heed. While some are reluctant to take up new responsibilities, others are too eager. We sometimes imagine that we can solve any problem and bear any responsibility. We want God to give us impressive callings and impressive visions. Unwilling to submit ourselves to God's process and timing, we rush into the world determined to do it by our own efforts and talents.

So, let me give you a word of warning. Do not despise small beginnings. Do not let yourself be overwhelmed by the task ahead. God will not give a vision or calling for which He can't equip you. But God may take more time preparing you than you would like. There may be several seasons of growth and change required. One seed only produces one plant in the proper season. That plant can produce many seeds to plant in the right season. If you plant those in time, you will have a garden full of fruit and seeds for the future.

It takes time; do not despise the one small seed. By His process of creation and change, God will not only give you seed for the future but will shape you into the person you need to be to accomplish the calling He's given you. Do not get restless or dissatisfied. Do not grow impatient. Recognize that God is at work. It often turns out that what God has called you to is simpler than you may think, because you are working *with* God, not *for* Him. You are operating in His timing, not yours. God is calling you to trust His process. He is calling you to steward what He has already given you. He is asking you to keep planting seed.

I have often faced the temptation of rushing ahead of God's process. Early in my pastoral ministry, as our small church finally began to grow, I was convinced I had unlocked the secret. I believed we were on the fast-track to growth. I thought the process was over. I had broken through to a new level and thought I would continue to move forward. I thought I had finally become what I needed to be and knew what I needed to know. I looked at my growing congregation and thought that the number of people in front of me were the fruit of all my hard work.

That is how we often feel about positive change. We want God's process to be as short as possible, and the moment we begin to see change, we hope we're done with the process and can finally start enjoying all the rewards. With that thought in my head, God spoke something strange to me. God said, *Your people are not the fruit of your ministry; they are seed for the future.* I didn't understand what God meant.

So, God began to explain it to me. The results I was experiencing were not proof or validation of what I was doing. The growth of my church was not a reward for the work I had done. The new people God was bringing were the results of a long process, but they were also, and just as importantly, seeds for future things God wanted to do.

I began to recognize that fruit and seed are directly related. Fruit grows as the result of a process, but inside that fruit are the seeds of another God-ordained process and future growth. That is how God's process always works. As we reach the end, we find a new beginning. The results of God's process are how He begins anew. But we must be willing to plant the seed again. Just as God had commanded Adam and Eve to be fruitful and multiply, so He calls us to take what is given and invest it toward future things. We are changed so that we might give. The harvest of new believers is to be celebrated, then discipled. They must continue to be given new revelation and a healthy atmosphere.

Once I learned this lesson, it changed the way I thought about my work and what I was receiving from God. New people were no longer the measurement of my success, but an opportunity to see God do more new things and the evidence of new seasons ahead. Every conclusion was a new beginning. And that produced new faith. What I received was not the end. Suddenly, I had faith to see each end with a vision for still greater things to come. By faith, everything given is the seed for greater things to come.

This trust allowed Jesus to promise Nathanael that he would see still greater things. As Jesus famously told His disciples in John 14:12, "Whoever believes in me will do the works I have been doing, and they will do even greater things than these." So, our faith grows as God continues to rework His process in our lives.

Whatever change God is working in us is also our new beginning. And it's not just for us. He has worked this change so that we might serve and bless others. God saves us so that we might share that salvation. He heals us so that we may lay hands on the sick and pray for the healing of others. He has taught us His Word so that we might teach it to others. Whatever God is doing in us, He is doing it as seed planted to bless others. He is still commanding us to be fruitful and multiply.

What We Have to Give

Adam and Eve's disobedience sacrificed the calling God had given them. Instead of stewarding creation, they became self-centered and worked to make themselves like God. Out of selfish interest, they neglected the work God had given them. After receiving all of creation in its complete goodness, they refused to participate in caring for it. Instead, they demanded more. They sacrificed what God had freely given and the calling He had offered them. So, God began another process of restoring what had been lost.

After Jesus' resurrection, having given them His life, He tasked His followers with a new calling. He commanded them to go into all the world and make disciples. In many ways, it was a renewal of the calling Adam and Eve had lost. Jesus' followers were to subdue the earth through the power of the Spirit and the word of their testimony. Jesus' followers would now rule with Him through the preaching of His gospel.

Much had been given to them, and much was required. But that new calling must have seemed completely overwhelming as they watched Jesus disappear into the clouds. How could a handful of common men and women change the world? But they obeyed Jesus. They prayed, waited, and trusted His timing. They knew God's process was at work. They waited until the Holy Spirit fell and empowered them with new boldness.

The Church followed the Spirit's work of revelation. Knowing that transformation begins with revelation, the apostles followed the revelation of God. On the day of Pentecost, Peter stood up and declared the work and ministry of Jesus (see Acts 2). The crowd responded with, "What must we do?" Peter knew they were experiencing new revelation. Just a month and a half previously, they had called for the crucifixion of Jesus. Now they were asking how to receive His salvation. Later, when Peter was called to the house of a gentile, he recognized that they were experiencing a new revelation from God. He, a Jew, became willing to participate with God in the work to which he had been called and empowered.

What Peter and others received became the seed for what came next. One process led to another, and that became the empowerment for still greater work. Seed grew into fruit that produced seed for a new movement. You and I are the beneficiaries of their work and obedience. And so, it also falls to us to take up that work and continue.

There is a powerful story in the early chapters of Acts— perhaps just a few days after the believers had received the Spirit—that illustrates the point. Peter and John were going up to the temple to pray. On their way, they were interrupted by a lame beggar outside the temple gate. The lame man asked Peter and John for money. Peter's response has always moved me. Peter said to the man, "Silver or gold I do not have [access to] but what I do have [possess] I give you. In the name of Jesus Christ of Nazareth, walk" (Acts 3:6). The man did. The lame man got up and followed them into the temple, jumping and worshiping God.

What did Peter and John have? They didn't have wealth. They didn't have gold or silver. They didn't have worldly power or political influence. By the world's standards, they didn't have much. But they possessed what God had given them. What they had was the revelation of a divine opportunity and the authority to fulfill it. They had a power and authority far greater than the world's. And the lame man received far more than he could have imagined.

Peter and John gave what they had. That is exactly what God is asking of you. That's all. He isn't asking for you to be anything other than what He is making you. But He is asking you to live out the revelation He is giving you and to give away what you have received. It may not look like much to the world, and it may not impress many people, but God can use what you have to do miraculous things. God is simply looking for people who will trust His process and give back what has been given to them. Or as Jesus commanded His first disciples as He sent them out to the surrounding towns, "Freely you have received; freely give" (Matthew 10:8).

What do you have? What has God given you? What do you see? How can what you have received be planted as a seed for still greater things? Where is God giving you new responsibility? Where has God given you authority? If God is working His process of change in your life, you can be sure there will be new things for you to give. Do you possess the faith to see it? Can you recognize that what you have been given is just the beginning of what God wants to do?

God's culminating act of creating humanity was not the end of His creative process. It was the beginning of the work He wanted to do with Adam and Eve. God chooses to work with you, too. Let your faith grow. Recognize whatever talent, gift, or strength you have as the seed being planted to change the world. That is how God wants to do it. We don't need riches. We don't need to become celebrities. We don't need complex plans. What God is looking for are humble men and women who will trust His process and sow the seed He gives them. Just faith, even the size of a mustard seed.

Embrace what God is doing. Take up the authority of the task He has given. Bear the responsibility. And give as you have received.

Remember this: Whoever sows sparingly will also reap sparingly, and whoever sows generously will also reap generously.

2 Corinthians 9:6

PHASE 7

Rest

By the seventh day God had finished the work he had been doing; so on the seventh day he rested from all his work.

—Genesis 2:2

On the seventh and final day of creation, God rested. For six days, He had moved His creation through each stage of the process. For six days, His creative work formed and shaped the world into being. For six days, He spoke new things into existence. But on the last day, God simply rested. It's one of the most unique features of the creation story. God took a whole day to rest. God's process ends with Sabbath.

Was God tired? Had His work finally worn Him out? No. Sabbath is far more than rest from exhaustion. It is more than resting from the weariness of our work. Sabbath rest was designed by God as a part of His creative process. Psalm 121 promises that God never slumbers or sleeps;

however, on the final day of His creative work, He did take a Sabbath. Rest was practiced by God as a reminder to us of its importance. We neglect it too often, and in so doing, we short-cut God's full creative work in our lives.

Perhaps it is surprising to you how important the theme of Sabbath rest is throughout the Bible. You see it here in the days of creation, but it continues to appear throughout the biblical story. Fresh out of Egyptian captivity, making their way through the wilderness, God stopped His people at the mountain and gave them His law. Alongside His commands not to worship idols or murder one another was the command, "Remember the Sabbath day by keeping it holy" (Exodus 20:8). In Exodus 20, the Sabbath commandment has one of the longest explanations of any of the Ten Commandments. And God commanded Israel to keep a Sabbath because He had kept one. Verse 11 records, "For in six days the LORD made the heavens and the earth, the sea, and all that is in them, but he rested on the seventh day."

Israel was not always faithful in keeping a Sabbath. The prophets often criticized the people for working on that holy day. Even after their return from exile, Nehemiah was shocked to see the streets full and the markets open on the Sabbath. Everywhere people were carrying heavy loads and paying no attention to God's command for rest. What is so hard about rest? What is it that constantly tempted God's people to work? Why do we find it so difficult to keep a Sabbath?

It is not easy to stop. It's not in our nature. It feels as though we are wasting time, falling behind, and missing out. When there is so much to be done—and there is always a lot to be done—we remain nervous about any time not spent making progress. Then, there is the unavoidable outcome of all that tireless work. We burn out, give up, and too often abandon the work altogether. We work until we can't. We strive until we're too tired to go on. We seem to understand nothing about God's teaching on the Sabbath. I think it is our lack of Sabbath understanding that makes us so reluctant to take one. The truth is, Sabbath is not wasted time. Sabbath is how God renews His creative work.

A Call to Remember

Keeping a Sabbath doesn't mean lying around doing nothing. Resting from our work does not mean turning off our minds. Sabbath is not wasting time. Instead, Sabbath is a critical part of how we mark what God has created in His process and how we prepare ourselves for new work ahead. I am convinced every believer should have a regular Sabbath. Go to church. Worship with other believers. Take a day off.

But I want to talk to you about another kind of Sabbath. Just as the ancient Israelites kept a regular Sabbath of years, we need Sabbath seasons in which we take the time to recognize what God has been doing in our lives, families, and churches. That happens weekly, but often, we need a more extended season to be still and recognize what God has been doing.

In the creation account of Genesis, the Sabbath was preceded by God taking the time to see all that He had created. "God saw all that he had made, and it was very good. And there was evening, and there was morning," and so, Genesis concludes, "Thus the heavens and the earth were completed in all their vast array" (1:31–2:1). Having finished His work, God was not done. The final stage of His process was to see what had been accomplished and to rest in its goodness. Sabbath is a part of the process.

God did not enter His Sabbath collapsing onto His heavenly hammock with His eyes closed and muscles fatigued. He entered His Sabbath observing and enjoying all that He had done. He entered His Sabbath with joy, not exhaustion. That is the kind of Sabbath of which we need more.

There is a danger in a book like this. We have spent several chapters talking about work, talking about action, and talking about God doing new things in our lives and churches. We could start to think that every day must be a day of new work. We could want every day to be about some great change. While there are many days in which God calls us into this work with faithful determination, if we are not careful, we can lose our perspective on what God is doing.

That is not how God entered His rest. He took His Sabbath with the satisfaction of what had been done. After a hard day of yard work or after hours of painting a room in our homes, for example, we all step back and want to see what we have accomplished. There are few things more satisfying than a hard day's work and the results from it. We might be tired, but we feel good having accomplished something. So, too, God stepped back and saw that everything He had made was good, and He took the time to rest in it.

When was the last time you had that kind of Sabbath? When was the last time you took the time to examine what God has been doing in your life? I don't mean a half hour of prayer or a Sunday service. But when was the last time you took real time simply to appreciate what God has done? When was the last time you found rest in it?

While Sabbath was first commanded by God at the mountain in Exodus 20 just before Israel entered the promised land, God reminded His people that they would still need a Sabbath once they took possession of that land. Moses, preaching to the people in the book of Deuteronomy, turned their attention to the topic. Moses commanded them, "Observe the Sabbath day by keeping it holy, as the LORD your God has commanded you" (5:12). And Moses went on to lay out the prohibitions. They were not to do work, and they were not to allow their sons, daughters, or servants to do work. Not even their livestock was to work. But in that sermon, Moses went further. He reminded them why: "Remember that you were slaves in Egypt and that the LORD your God brought you out of there with a mighty hand and an outstretched arm" (5:15).

Do you see what Moses did? He not only told them why God had commanded the Sabbath, but he modeled what they should do with it. The Sabbath existed to help them remember. They were to practice a Sabbath so that they would not forget what God had done for them. The Sabbath reminded them of how God had saved them from being slaves. God intended their Sabbath to be a time of reflection and remembering. God had been faithful to them in the past and would be again in the future.

But the Sabbath is also a warning. We are commanded to remember because we are prone to forget. We are prone to forget what God has done for us. Even now, no matter where you are in this process of God's creative work in your life, no matter how great the miracles you have seen, you are prone to forget. What Israelite would have thought it possible to forget the parted waters, or the pillar of fire and smoke, or the plagues that came over Egypt? But according to Moses' final sermon, forgetting was what they were most at risk of doing. "Remember," Moses commanded them. That is what the Sabbath was for.

I can't help wondering what you might be overlooking. What things has God done that you have forgotten? In the busyness of new work, new goals, and new visions, is it possible you have forgotten what God has done in your past? Has your forgetfulness of His faithfulness weakened the faith you have for today?

Building Your Faith

The temptation we face at each stage of God's process is forgetting what God has already done and fearing what might lie ahead. We forget the previous day's work and live in the fear of tomorrow. When we fail to remember God's past faithfulness, we are left unsure of His future faithfulness. Remembering God's works is also for the purpose of building our faith for what He will do in the future. We do well to remind ourselves that He is the same God, yesterday, today, and forever (see Hebrews 13:8).

Sabbath is one of God's best tools for helping us remember. But Sabbath takes faith. It takes faith to stop working. It takes faith to recognize that a season of rest is not wasted time. It takes faith to wait on the Lord. When I was a pastor, I often spoke about what God was doing and what He was calling our church to do. I cast a vision and encouraged people to take up the work. Most days, I had a pretty good answer about what God was doing and what He was asking us to do. But there are days when we must stop. There are days when He does not call us to go, but rather to wait, to rest, and to tarry. There are times He wants our attention not on things ahead but on things accomplished.

Do you remember the scene of the first Christians gathered in the upper room praying? They had been given a great task. They were to go into all the world and make disciples. That was a big vision. My mind immediately wants to start preparing and praying for the vision forward. But before Jesus' disciples were allowed to go, Jesus commanded them to wait. They were to wait in Jerusalem until they received power. Think of all the times God's people are made to wait. The dark night in which the Egyptian slaves waited out the Passover. The days spent marking time in the wilderness. The prolonged circling and waiting for the walls of Jericho to crumble. The days in which Christ's body lay awaiting resurrection in the tomb.

Each moment of waiting requires a serious commitment of faith. Waiting tests our faith, but it also builds our faith. As we wait, our anticipation builds. As we wait, we remember what God has done before. As we tarry, we find faith for new things. The Bible promises that as we wait, we receive more of God and find our confidence bolstered.

The psalmist wrote, "Be still, and know that I am God" (Psalm 46:10). And remember the psalmist's other words, "Wait for the LORD; be strong and take heart and wait for the LORD" (27:14). Isaiah 40:31 promised, "Those who hope in the LORD will renew their strength. They will soar on wings like eagles; they will run and not grow weary, they will walk and not be faint." Or Jeremiah wrote in his Lamentations, "The LORD is good to those who wait for him, to the soul who seeks him" (3:25 ESV).

I hope that reading those verses builds your faith. Reading them builds mine. It reminds me that time spent waiting and remembering the faithfulness of God is never time wasted. This is, I think, the real power of a Sabbath. Sabbath is God's way of helping us appreciate what He has done, and at the same time, it is a tool for building our faith in what He wants to do next. Without taking the time to stop and wait, our appreciation of things past and our faith for things future are both diminished.

We have come to an important moment in this book and an opportunity to do what God has commanded. I want you to use this final chapter as an invitation to think back over each of the days of creation. Remember the way God has been working His creative process in your life. Perhaps it is things He did long ago, or perhaps things you are experiencing right now, but in each day of God's work, there is a reminder of His faithfulness and a seed planted for what He is preparing to do next.

Just as God reached the end of His process and looked back on the days of His work, seeing that His creation was good, this is an opportunity to recognize the good He is doing in your life.

1. Do you remember the darkness and chaos that once characterized your life?
2. Do you remember how the light of God's revelation spoke life into you and cast a vision for what He wanted to do in you?

3. Can you see the way He began to change the atmosphere of your situation, bringing new people, gifts, and calling into your life?

4. Do you see the way He taught you new structures? How He taught you to discipline and order your life through the wisdom of His Word?

5. Can you look back and see the critical seasons He orchestrated? Seasons of growth and loss, seasons of rest and reaping?

6. And can you see the additions? Can you see the new things that have formed in your life through His faithfulness and work?

7. Do you remember the opposition? Do you remember how, through that opposition, God matured your faith and taught you to trust Him in battles and storms?

8. And when was the last time you stopped long enough to remember it all? When was the last time you rested long enough for your faith to be built by all that God has done?

Stepping back from His creation, God saw that it was good. Can you see that it is good? Can you see that what God has been doing in your life has been good? I know it may not be perfect. There may still be struggles, opposition, and unanswered prayers, but do you see how He has been working? Does that not build your faith for what He will continue to do in the future?

Whatever you see looking back on your time with God, know that He is not done. You are here because He is continuing to work in your life. This moment of pause to remember is just the beginning of more God wants to do.

God's process is a repeating cycle. We are not called to one Sabbath, but to a repeating rhythm of them. So, too, God's creative work continues a constantly new cycle. Each repeating Sabbath builds our faith to receive a new word of revelation from God. That is where the process always starts. In the stillness and silence, God speaks a new word. He offers us a new promise. He lets us see new things still to come. On the Sabbath, a seed is planted for a new process, and another cycle of God's creative work in our lives begins to form.

The best place to receive a new word from God is not the finish line or some pinnacle of our success. The best place to receive a new word from God is in the still, quiet waiting of another Sabbath. This can be that moment. I believe this ending is really another new beginning.

Stop what you are doing. Quiet your heart. Remember what God has done for you before. Worship Him again. Cast your cares on Him. Wait. And ask the Holy Spirit— the same Spirit that hovered over the dark and chaotic waters before creation—to speak to you again. He will.

Who knows what God will say? Only He knows what He has in store for you in the days ahead. Wait on Him. Trust His process and see what new things He wants to create in you.

> Then God blessed the seventh day and made it holy.
> Genesis 2:3

NOTES

Chapter 2 Chaos and Darkness

1. Stanley M. Horton, *What the Bible Says about the Holy Spirit* (Springfield, MO: Gospel Publishing House, 1976), 52.

Chapter 3 Phase 1

1. *Encountering God Study Bible: Insights from Blackaby Ministries on Living Our Faith* (New York: Thomas Nelson, 2023), 670.

2. Emerging Technology, "How Far Can the Human Eye See a Candle Flame?," *MIT Technology Review,* July 31, 2015, https://www.technologyreview.com/2015/07/31/72658/how-far-can-the-human-eye-see-a-candle-flame/.

Chapter 4 Phase 2

1. NASA Science Editorial Team, "The Atmosphere: Earth's Security Blanket," *NASA,* October 02, 2019, https://science.nasa.gov/earth/earth-atmosphere/the-atmosphere-earths-security-blanket/.

2. The Alternative Board, "Culture Eats Strategy for Breakfast," The Alternative Board Blog, February 26, 2020, https://www.thealternativeboard.com/blog/culture-eats-strategy.

Acknowledgments

Since I first began to recognize the importance of God's process in Genesis, I have taught it across the nation to hundreds of ministers, ministries, and churches. I have repeatedly been asked to put that teaching into writing as a book. Doing so has taken a team and has been largely motivated by so many of those personal encouragements and proddings. For everyone who has encouraged me to take on this work, I owe you my first thanks.

To my wife, Rita DuBose, who has heard me teach on this topic more than anyone else, I also want to say thank you. She has been the most faithful voice in encouraging me to complete this book. I want to thank her for her support and patience, especially. She has listened to me talk about these ideas over and over, and each time, she has heard them with genuine interest and encouragement. She has helped me refine so much of this material, and I hope my work has achieved what she has long believed in.

Of all those who have encouraged me to write this book, the Assemblies of God District Superintendent

Bill Wilson's wife, Joy Wilson, has been one of the most compelling. She appointed herself to be my life coach and has repeatedly asked me, "Rick, why haven't you put this into a book?" She has not stopped *coaching* me in this direction. And I look forward to placing one of the first signed copies into her hands. Thank you, Joy, for continuing to ask.

Finally, I must also say thank you to Chase Replogle. Chase helped me develop my last book, *In Jesus' Name*. He did so well with it that I asked him to help me with this book as well. He is a genius at crafting sermon notes and ideas I formed through speaking into something readable. Chase, your ability to form ideas into understandable words on paper is amazing. Thanks for the hours you gave to this book and the heart you have put into it.

RICK DUBOSE is the assistant general superintendent of the Assemblies of God and a member of the executive leadership team. The author of *In Jesus' Name* and *The Church That Works*, DuBose is a respected pastor and has served the Assemblies of God in various local and national leadership positions for more than two decades. He and his wife, Rita, have three adult children and eight grandsons and make their home in Springfield, Missouri.

CONNECT WITH RICK:

 @Rick.DuBose.56

@RichardWDuBose

@RevRDuBose